★ REFLECTIONS OF A ★
BLACK COWBOY

BOOK TWO ★ THE BUFFALO SOLDIERS

★ REFLECTIONS OF A ★
BLACK COWBOY

BY ROBERT H. MILLER

ILLUSTRATED BY RICHARD LEONARD

SILVER BURDETT PRESS

Published by Silver Burdett Press, Inc., a division of Simon & Schuster, Inc.,
Prentice Hall Bldg., Englewood Cliffs, NJ 07632.
Designed by Leslie Bauman
Manufactured in the United States of America
10   9   8   7   6   5   4   3   2   1

Library of Congress Cataloging-in-Publication Data

Miller, Robert H. (Robert Henry)
Reflections of a Black cowboy.
Includes bibliographical references (p. 87)
Contents: bk. 1. Cowboys—bk. 2. The Buffalo soldiers.
1. Afro-American cowboys—West (U.S.)—Biography—Juvenile literature.
2. West (U.S.)—Biography—Juvenile literature.   3. West (U.S.)—Social life
and customs—Juvenile literature.   4. Cowboys.   5.
Afro-Americans—Biography.   6. West (U.S.)—Biography.
I. Title.
F596.M646   1990
978' .00496073022 B
ISBN 0-382-24080-4 (lib. bdg.)   ISBN 0-382-24085-5 (pbk.)   90-8661

TO MY HERO

My mother, Margaret Boyd, for her spirit, courage, wisdom, and undying belief that tomorrow means nothing unless you do something today.

CONTENTS

PREFACE

Welcome to *Reflections of a Black Cowboy*. The books in this series were written to introduce you, the young reader, to African-American people who helped settle the West. You'll meet cowboys, pioneers, soldiers, scouts, and mail drivers, and be a part of history as our narrator the "Old Cowboy" remembers some stories from days gone by.

As young boys, my brother John and I would sit on the floor around my mother's favorite chair, waiting quietly for her to read us a story. She liked to read to us about faraway places and magical times. When I closed my eyes, I could see myself in the story—as a bystander or one of the main characters or often as the hero.

Like many black children growing up in the fifties, my heroes were drawn from the movies. Many of my favorite movies were westerns. Judging from what I saw in these movies, I figured there were no black cowboys. In the movies, most blacks had roles in the background as cooks or shoeshine boys or stable hands. Unfortunately, those weren't exactly the roles I had in mind for myself when I strapped on my play gun and holster outfit.

It was after one of those games of Cowboys and Indians that my mother told John and me a few new stories about her uncles, Ed and Joe Cloud. We thought ''Cloud'' was a strange-sounding name. Our mother explained that our great uncles were cowboys who had traveled throughout Texas and Mexico. Often, they had to shoot their way out of trouble on cattle drives.

From that day on, John and I had a different perspective when we played our games of Cowboys and Indians. Instead of Hollywood movie stars, our uncles became our heroes.

This book is an effort to help define our cultural heritage and to pay tribute to Ed and Joe Cloud and all the other black men and women who helped tame the West.

Journey back with me now to that place called the wild, wild West, where you can be whoever *you* want. All you need is a fast horse, some boots, and a saddle. Now close your eyes—enjoy the ride!

Robert H. Miller

INTRODUCTION

Researching this book was a struggle. There is so much information on African-American soldiers and their contributions to settling the West, I didn't know where to start. I wanted to choose events and people that I felt best represented the sterling careers of America's unsung heroes, the Buffalo Soldiers.

What amazed me was the lack of information on the subject in high school history books and elementary school social studies texts. It defies the imagination how these books can feature the history of the great ''Western Frontier'' and not mention the African-American soldier's contribution to settling that part of our country. It's like talking about great American baseball players and mentioning Joe

DiMaggio and Babe Ruth, but not Jackie Robinson, Willie Mays, or Hank Aaron.

Consequently, I have written this book to enlighten young readers about the history of the West. Americans from many different ethnic groups answered the call to adventure and duty. Those who served in the army perhaps answered the highest call of anyone. These men put their lives on the line in the service of their country. Of these, none performed more bravely than the Buffalo Soldiers.

This book is an effort to set the record straight about the contributions of the African-American soldier to the settlement of the West and America's drive to become a world power. From the Revolutionary War to Vietnam, African Americans have fought gallantly, many giving their lives, in every major war that involved the sovereignty of the United States. In spite of this fine record of performance, African Americans rarely were rewarded for their services, and their contributions have been at best only grudgingly acknowledged. This neglect was particularly bad in the nineteenth century during the Civil War, the Indian wars, and the Spanish-American War—the time of the Buffalo Soldier.

Whenever this country needed the finest fighting men she could find, she called on her best, the men of the Ninth and Tenth Cavalries, the Buffalo Soldiers. This book is a salute to those men, who endured the wrath of their enemies as well as injustices from the insensitive white people they were paid to protect. I also salute those brave white officers who led the Buffalo Soldiers into battle and understood their courage and their plight, for they are also worthy of recognition.

By having the character of the Old Cowboy narrate the stories to his dog, Sundown, I tried to create a storytelling atmosphere which also allows readers to place themselves in the midst of the action. I think you'll enjoy these stories, and

I hope they make you ask more questions about what really happened during the development of the West and what significant roles other African Americans played.

Now find your favorite easy chair and get ready to go on a western adventure with Sundown and the Old Cowboy.

CLOSE CALLS

The Old Cowboy had been walking for a long time with his dog, Sundown, trotting patiently along at his side. Finally, the Old Cowboy stopped. He smiled and nodded. Sundown stopped, too, and looked up at the Old Cowboy expectantly.

"If my memory serves me right, Sundown, it ought to be right over there, near that clump of tall pine trees at the edge of the forest," said the Old Cowboy. He untied his bandanna and wiped the sweat off his forehead. It was a hot summer day. The midday sun blazed down on them from high in the sky, and a warm, swift wind ruffled the leaves of the trees and swayed the tall prairie grasses.

The Old Cowboy and Sundown had been on the trail of a

secret place they'd heard about from a young Indian boy. Their search had led them from Montana to South Dakota.

"It is true, I swear it. My father's father told me of it when I was much smaller," the Indian boy had told the Old Cowboy. "He said to follow the wind where the air smells sweet and you'll see big cats and white water. It is where my people go to talk to the Great One."

The Old Cowboy had listened carefully. He'd lived in the Montana mountains for years and had mingled with many Indians there. He was pretty sure that the only place where the air smelled sweet and mountain lions were the size of buffalo, was the area he'd heard other Indians talk about. They had also said it was a place where the wind blows like a fast young pony. Judging from those stories, all signs pointed to South Dakota.

The Old Cowboy had to find this place, not because of the rumors of treasure buried there, but because something even more precious could be found here—words written in a language not even the Indians understood. The legend says that, "Whoever can read these words will be enlightened." The Old Cowboy felt a tingle of excitement as he began to walk toward the forest.

Nobody really knew where the Old Cowboy came from. It was said that he had arrived in this country on a slave ship many years before. That was the time when Africans were taken from their villages in Africa and brought here to be sold as slaves to white people. Some people heard that the Old Cowboy had lived in Montana before it had become a state, but nobody was sure where he had been before or how he had made his way out there. Everybody who met this old fellow knew he was different. He seemed to be able to communicate with your spirit, almost as if he could read your mind. The Old Cowboy was like this because he was a man who followed his dreams. And now he was about to have another dream realized.

As the Old Cowboy climbed over a large fallen tree, he knew he was getting close.

"You smell that boy? That air sure smells mighty sweet to me!" the Old Cowboy said to Sundown. The dog barked in agreement. The two of them finally reached a spot described to them by the Indian boy. The Old Cowboy halted and pondered a narrow path that led to a fork in the road.

"Be careful when you come to the 'chicken' feet path," the boy had said. "You must go to the left side down a short road. There you will see tall trees. Near the trees is a big rock shaped like the face of a man."

"Come on, Sundown, this way, boy," said the Old Cowboy as he started down the path.

Sundown raced ahead of the Old Cowboy figuring a road was a road.

"Slow up, Sundown!" the Cowboy shouted anxiously. He had a feeling there was danger ahead. But Sundown had a mind of his own sometimes, and he raced smack dab into a pool of quicksand. The Old Cowboy knew that quicksand is a very dangerous pool of sand and water that has no bottom. The more you struggle to get out, the farther down you sink, until you're buried alive.

The Old Cowboy hurried over to the edge of the quicksand pool. By now the sand was starting to rise around Sundown's neck.

"Don't move, Sundown," the Old Cowboy ordered sharply. "Stay still!"

Sundown whimpered a little, but something in the Cowboy's voice made him stay as still as a rock. The Old Cowboy looked around quickly. He needed to find something that would help him pull his trusted friend from the deadly pool.

Now the sand had moved close to Sundown's mouth. The Old Cowboy spotted a loose branch. He ripped it off the tree and stripped it of its leaves. Then he took off his belt and tied it to the branch. He swung the stick out to Sundown, who was just able to bite into it.

"That a boy. Hang on, Sundown!" the Old Cowboy said encouragingly. He pulled on the belt with all his might. Sundown slowly came out of the quicksand. When his front paws were on solid ground at the edge of the pool, he pulled himself completely out. He wasn't hurt, but he was shaking like a leaf.

"Come on over here, boy, that's a good boy," said the Old Cowboy. He gently wiped the dirt off his old friend and patted him soothingly.

"I guess we better go around this pool, what do you think?" the Old Cowboy said to Sundown.

The dog wagged his tail. He knew he'd better stick close to the Old Cowboy this time and not run off again.

The two friends carefully made their way around that pool of quicksand and continued to roam the forest. Soon they reached a group of tall pine trees.

"Come on, boy," the Old Cowboy said excitedly to Sundown. "We've found it."

But when they got to the trees the Old Cowboy didn't find what he had been looking for—a big rock shaped like a man's face. He scratched his head. "Now I'm sure I remember everything that Indian boy told me," he said in a puzzled voice. He looked around again. Suddenly he spotted a clearing about fifteen feet away. On either side of the clearing were trees whose branches bent over to form a canopy.

"It's got to be over there, boy," he said with a nod. Sundown followed the Old Cowboy over to the clearing. The Old Cowboy looked behind a large tree and there it was, staring right back at him—a large stone head shaped like that of an African man. He knew it was African because of the broad nose and lips, and it looked like the carvings he had seen as a child, long ago. It looked very old.

The Old Cowboy gazed at the stone head. As he did, many questions began to run through his mind. Who had carved this face? The Old Cowboy knew that the ancestors of the Indians had come to America from Asia centuries before the European explorers. There were reports that Africans had come here centuries ago, too. Had one of those Africans carved this face? Or had it been made by a former slave? Was the head a symbol of an African people's past? The Old Cowboy continued to study the carvings.

"Where's them words the Indian boy told me about," the cowboy muttered as he ran his hands over the smooth surface of the head. Then he noticed that some words had been carved into the back of the head.

"This must be what the Indian boy was talking about," said the Old Cowboy. Sundown sat back on his haunches and watched as the Old Cowboy rubbed the dirt away and looked at the carvings carefully.

"These ain't words, Sundown," he said finally. "They're little pictures. And it looks like they tell a story."

As the Old Cowboy studied the pictures, he lost track of time. The sun had begun to set when Sundown caught the scent of a nearby animal. Sundown's growl was as low as a whisper, and the Old Cowboy didn't hear it.

"I think I got it figured out, Sundown," said the unsuspecting Cowboy. "I know what the pictures say."

Sundown didn't move, but his growl got louder. Then he began to bark ferociously.

The Old Cowboy jerked up his head and saw the biggest grizzly bear of his entire life coming toward them. The grizzly stood up on its hind legs. It was at least twelve feet tall.

"Come on, boy, we'd better git like the wind now!" shouted the Old Cowboy. He turned to run away from the bear, but he tripped over a rock and fell to the ground. At the same moment, he felt the weight of the huge grizzly on top of him.

"Sundown, help!" the Old Cowboy screamed desperately as he tried to wrestle out of the bear's grasp.

Sundown heard his master's voice and raced over to him. The dog was determined to save his best friend. He gave a mighty leap and sunk his sharp teeth in the bear's nose. The grizzly howled in pain and jumped back. Then he ran into the woods as if someone had lit a fire under him. Sundown followed the bear a few feet into the forest and barked at him warningly.

The Old Cowboy sat up slowly. He was feeling tired and sore.

"That a boy, Sundown, look at him run," he called out. "You can come back here now."

Sundown trotted over to his friend. The Old Cowboy scratched him behind his ears and said, "You saved my life this time, big fella. That makes us even."

The Old Cowboy looked at the sky. It was getting dark, and he decided to camp in the clearing. "That old head ain't going nowhere, and lord knows I could use some shut-eye."

He made a campfire and laid out his bedroll. Then he cooked up some grub for him and Sundown to eat. After dinner, the Old Cowboy settled in by the fire with Sundown curled up next to him. After coming this far, the Old Cowboy was glad to have found the giant African stone head, and he was happy that he had figured out the pictures carved on it. They told the story of the struggle of proud Africans in this country and their hopes and dreams of the future.

The Old Cowboy slept. But he kept one eye open and one hand resting gently on his rifle. He knew he had the right to be there, and no grizzly bear was going to scare him off.

EMANUEL STANCE, THE FIRST BLACK SOLDIER TO RECEIVE THE MEDAL OF HONOR

The Old Cowboy woke at dawn. He yawned and stretched. Then he saw that Sundown was nosing into his knapsack. The mutt pulled out a sandwich wrapped in paper.

"Okay, okay, boy," the Old Cowboy said with a laugh. "Come over here and I'll unwrap it for you."

After they both had eaten some breakfast and drunk cold, pure water from a nearby stream, the Old Cowboy filled his pipe and sat down under a tree opposite the face of the African head. The Old Cowboy was still a little sore from his run-in with the grizzly the afternoon before, so he decided to stay put that day. Besides, the carved rock reminded him of stories he knew about African

Americans, especially the stories about the brave men known as the Buffalo Soldiers.

"Sit here by me, Sundown," said the Old Cowboy. "I've got some stories to tell you."

Sundown was about to chase after a butterfly, but when he heard the Old Cowboy's voice, he came over and sat down next to him. The Old Cowboy puffed thoughtfully on his pipe for a moment. Then he began to speak.

After the Civil War, the West began to grow as fast as a young colt. Settlers by the thousands loaded up their covered wagons, formed wagon trains, and headed West. The cities of the East were becoming so crowded they were busting out at their seams like a fat hog after feeding time. People needed leg room to stretch out, and the West was the likeliest place to go. All those new arrivals thought about was getting there. It never dawned on them that the land they were claiming as theirs belonged to the Commanche, Kiowa, Cheyenne, and Apache Indians. Those settlers probably didn't think the Indians would mind them grabbing their sacred hunting and burial grounds and pushing them into little corners of land. But the Indians did mind, and trouble started brewing like a country stew, the kind you don't serve at the kitchen table.

The U.S. government and the army soon got word that the white settlers were having serious problems with the Indians. There were so many reports of raids on settlers by the Indians the government felt that something had to be done to protect them. Just one year and three months to the day after the Civil War, on July 28, 1866, Congress voted to add four all-black infantry regiments to the army. They were the twenty-fourth and twenty-fifth Infantry regiments, and the Ninth and Tenth Cavalries.

Some say the government had a couple of reasons for doing this. One reason was to get African Americans out of the eastern part of the country; others have said that the government was sending them out West to perform duties the white soldiers didn't want. But whatever the reason, during that time there were no black soldiers in the East, only on the western frontier.

After the Civil War, black people had a hard time finding work, even though they had died in large numbers and were partly responsible for the North's victory over the South. Still, nobody wanted to hire them, so when they heard about joining the army for thirteen dollars a month plus food and shelter, they signed up. Men who had been farmers or cooks in the South became willing to give up years of their lives to ride out West, a place they'd never been, to risk their lives for the safety of white people they never knew, and to fight against a people they never hated. These brave and courageous men soon earned the respect of the Indians they defeated—they were called the Buffalo Soldiers.

Many black soldiers earned Medals of Honor during those clashes with the Indians. But the first soldier to win that medal was a nineteen-year-old young man named Emanuel Stance, from Charleston, South Carolina.

"Boy, where you running off to?" asked Emanuel's mother.

"I'm signing up. The army is hiring, and I'm gonna be a soldier," replied an excited Emanuel, as he packed a small bag.

"You 'bout knee high to a cricket. Ain't no army gonna

hire no short black boy. Now stop all that foolishness, we got work to do right around here," his mother said sharply.

Emanuel was on the short side, standing only about five-feet-tall, and that might be stretching the measuring stick a bit. But he was determined to get into one of those army uniforms.

"But Mama, I can make thirteen dollars a month. Ain't no job around here pay that kind of money," pleaded Emanuel.

His mother knew he was right. The war was over, and black folks couldn't find worthwhile jobs if their lives depended on it, and sometimes they did. Most white folks didn't look too kindly on lending a helping hand to a black man who was down on his luck. Enlisting in this new army was an opportunity that little Emanuel and other blacks just couldn't pass up.

Emanuel stood barefoot before his mother. He wore a pair of raggedy pants she had made for him and a shirt that was two sizes too big. Emanuel's mother shook her head at the thought that her son wanted to run off to some godforsaken land and be a soldier.

After a moment, she sighed deeply and said, "Well, I suppose we could use the money. Lord knows ain't much for a young boy to do round here. So I guess you can go on and join that army. But you be mighty careful, Emanuel, you hear me?" she added in a worried voice.

"Oh, Mama, you gonna be proud of me. I'll send home half my pay. You'll see, I'm gonna be somebody," said an excited Emanuel.

"I'm already proud of you. Do as you're told but don't do nothing foolish you hear?" she said. Her eyes filled with tears of love and pride as she hugged her son for the last time.

Emanuel finished packing up what little belongings he had. He smiled at his mother and looked around the shack they lived in. Then he stepped out the door and started his long journey to New Orleans to enlist in the Ninth Cavalry of the U.S. Army.

When Emanuel arrived in New Orleans it didn't take him long to find out where to sign up. Every black man he saw was just as anxious to join this new army as he was. Emanuel asked around and just followed everybody else. It wasn't long before he, along with hundreds of other black men, were all standing in line to make thirteen dollars a month with no idea of the hardships that lay ahead of them. Of course, Emanuel wasn't thinking about that. All he could think about was wearing that blue army uniform and marching tall. He didn't fight in the Civil War, but he could remember how proud those black soldiers looked when they marched through Charleston, their backs straight and their heads held higher than an eagle can fly, all marching as if they were one man. He knew then that there was something about being a soldier that made you somebody—and Emanuel Stance wanted to be somebody.

Meanwhile, the two commanding officers watched the recruits as they signed up.

"Do you think this experiment, forming these two Cavalries will work, Colonel Hatch?" asked Major Morrow.

"It better work," replied the colonel. "Washington is banking on it."

"But look at them," said the major. "We've got to train these men and get them ready for combat in just a few weeks. Judging from the looks of them, it's going to be impossible."

"They had a pretty impressive record during the Civil

War,'' Colonel Hatch reminded the major. ''They've proved that they've got what it takes. They're eager to learn. I haven't seen white soldiers enlisting in such large numbers, have you major?''

Colonel Edward Hatch was in charge of the Ninth Regiment Cavalry, U. S. Colored Troops. He knew how important the successful preparation of these black soldiers for combat was to Washington. That was why he had carefully selected Maj. Albert Morrow for the task of recruiting and training them.

Major Morrow left the colonel and began to walk down the line of recruits. When he spotted little Emanuel Stance in line, the major couldn't believe his eyes. In fact he almost didn't see Emanuel standing between the two other men. He walked over to get a closer look, thinking that maybe one of the men had brought along his son. But as he got closer he saw a young man with a determined look in his eyes.

''What's your name, boy?'' asked the major.

''Emanuel Stance, sir!'' Emanuel shouted, with his chest stuck out farther than a peacock.

''How old are you?'' continued the major.

''Nineteen, sir,'' said Emanuel.

The major looked at him and nodded. He could see from Emanuel's attitude that even though he was short, he had the makings of a good soldier. Here was a man who wanted to be in the army. From past experience the major knew that this kind of desire was necessary, especially in battle. He continued checking the black recruits. There was no question that they were in top physical condition, except for Emanuel Stance, but he still worried whether the black soldier would stand and fight.

''Well, what do you think?'' asked Colonel Hatch when the major returned.

"We'll see how they do when they get to Fort McKavett for training," replied Major Morrow. "That Texas sun will determine if they've got the stuff to be soldiers."

Training at Fort McKavett under the hot sun was no picnic. From sunup to sundown, Major Morrow drilled his black troops. They marched in ranks, sometimes in the middle of the day, when the waves of heat were so deep you couldn't see the man in front of you. They rode their horses in more formations than there are stars in the sky and got so good at firing their rifles and pistols, not a man in any white infantry could challenge them. Texas was truly a test of a man's grit. General Sheridan, who had led one of the Union armies during the Civil War, once said, "If I owned Texas and hell, I'd rent out Texas and live in hell."

For the black soldier, Texas was tough alright, in more ways than one. Not only did he have to put up with the heat, marching, and riding in formations all day, he soon realized the army was as much against him as it was for him. The horses he rode were rejects from the all-white units; there were some from the famous Seventh Cavalry led by General George Armstrong Custer and others that were actually used during the Civil War. Each man would have to ride a worn-out horse into battle against Indians riding fresh young ponies. F Company, which was a part of the Ninth Cavalry, had forty-eight horses and forty-five of them were more than fifteen years old. Not only were the horses old and tired, many of the saddles and rifles were just as old. Often, the black soldiers had to scrape up ammunition like a hungry person hunts for food. But still their pride wouldn't let 'em quit.

As Major Morrow trained his troops, he felt their pride and determination. He began to feel sure that the Ninth Cavalry would become one of the finest groups of fighting men in the country. But little did he know that soon one of them would go down in history as the first black soldier to earn a Medal of Honor.

One day, Colonel Hatch called Major Morrow into his office.

"Major Morrow reporting as ordered, sir," said the major, saluting Colonel Hatch.

"Are your men ready for combat, major?" asked the colonel.

"I think so, sir," replied the major. "They've trained hard and well and from what I can see they're anxious to prove themselves."

The colonel nodded approvingly. "They'll get their chance first thing in the morning," he told the major. "You know we've had some problems with small bands of Kiowas and Comanches raiding our wagons and taking our horses. Well, last month they captured a wagon, tied the wagon master to the wheel, and set the wagon on fire. When a group of our men came to the rescue, they were overpowered, and Lieutenant Vincent was killed. Your assignment, major, is to take F Company to patrol the area above Fort Clark and along the Kickapoo River. I want to put an end to these raids."

"My men will get right on it, sir," replied the major.

"And, major, let me know how they perform," added the colonel. "I need the information for my report."

"Yes, sir," replied the major. He saluted smartly, turned, and left the office. He smiled a little as he walked back to his men. Tomorrow, many of them would get the chance to show their mettle.

That night at dinner, word had already slipped out that F Company was getting orders to ride out in the morning.

"You ready, little fella?" one of the soldiers asked Emanuel.

"I'm as ready as you, and you know it!" replied Emanuel. He had trained as hard as the other soldiers—maybe even harder. During his free time, he chopped wood and carried heavy equipment to build up his muscles. He ran as often as he could to build up his stamina. Emanuel's buddies were impressed by his efforts. They knew he had that little extra spark of determination that makes a person stand out.

"I's hear Indians can fight," said another soldier.

"Can't none of 'em whip me, ain't a man been born can whip me," said a muscular soldier who stood at least six foot three. He was right, too. This soldier had gotten into a fight with six white soldiers, not long ago. They'd been drinking, and they jumped him one evening just because he was black. When the dust settled, all six of the white soldiers either limped or were carried to sick bay. This black soldier was sentenced to the guard house for striking a white man. Yet, tomorrow he would risk his life fighting Indians to protect the lives of white settlers.

Early the next morning Major Morrow and a small scouting party of the Ninth Cavalry rode out of Fort McKavett looking for hostile Kiowas. Emanuel Stance was one of the soldiers in the party.

Kiowa raiding bands had been attacking wagon trains within twenty miles of the fort. About ten or twelve miles into their scouting mission, they spotted a small wagon train of settlers moving west. The major knew they needed protection, so he ordered his troops to ride down and escort them to the fort. No sooner had the order been given when they heard a strange noise that sounded like baby pigs squealing. Then they saw a band of about twenty Kiowas heading straight for that wagon train. The major gave the order to charge and like lightning busting from a bottle the F Company rode to the rescue.

Once the people in the wagon train realized they were under attack, the wagon master laid rawhide on those horses, and the race to safety was on.

"Left flank to the rear; right flank, follow me!" shouted the major.

Having been trained to act on command, the men immediately split up, leaving Emanuel in line to lead the left flank. The raiding party of Kiowas was gaining on the settlers, whose wagons were loaded down with every possession they owned. But the Ninth was gaining on the Kiowas. The soldiers galloped closer, they fired their rifles, and Kiowas began to fall like apples from a shaken tree.

The Kiowas suddenly realized that they were in a battle with a different kind of soldier. They too split up, one group riding on the left of the wagon train, and another group riding on the right. The major rode down hard at an angle, cutting off part of the raiding party that was starting to feel the losses of its men. Realizing a temporary defeat, the Kiowas broke ranks and galloped away.

"After them," shouted Major Morrow. As soon as they heard the order, Emanuel and his men gallantly gave chase after the Kiowas, firing their rifles until it was clear the Indians were really retreating. They had had enough for that day. Then Emanuel and the other soldiers returned to the wagon train to await further orders.

"You and your men arrived just in the nick of time, major," said the wagon master gratefully. "We'd all be killed if it weren't for you."

"Where are you headed?" asked Major Morrow.

"We're going to Fort McKavett to get supplies," replied

the wagon master. "Then we plan to settle down around Kickapoo Springs."

"We'll escort you as far as the fort," Major Morrow told him. "But after that, you're on your own. I'd be careful if I were you," continued the major. "Kickapoo Springs is still rather hostile."

He turned to his men and gave the order to divide ranks. Providing cover on both sides of the wagon, the F Company escorted the wagon train safely back to Fort McKavett. The soldiers had passed their first test in battle by facing a fierce group of Kiowa Indians.

"Well, major, how did they do?" Colonel Hatch asked Major Morrow a short time later.

"I think we've got one of the bravest and best-trained group of men I've ever seen in battle," the major replied promptly. "One soldier in particular showed himself to be a natural-born leader."

"Which soldier?" the colonel wanted to know.

"His name is Emanuel Stance," answered the major. "I gave the order to charge after some runaway Kiowas, and without hesitation, he took off after them with just a few men. And let me tell you, sir," the major added excitedly, "in all my years of service I've never seen shooting like these men shoot. They aim, and whatever they point at, they hit."

Colonel Hatch smiled at the major, "So I can report to Washington that so far this experiment is a success?"

"Sir, I'd consider it an honor to lead them in battle again," the major replied. "And furthermore, I want to recommend that Emanuel Stance be promoted to corporal for what he did today."

The colonel nodded. "Put that in your report, major, and I'll see that it's done," he said.

For the next three years, Emanuel Stance fought bravely during many skirmishes with raiding Indians. He had risen to the rank of sergeant and was highly respected by his men.

Around May 20, 1870, Capt. Henry Carroll, Sergeant Stance, and a small detachment of men were out looking for some U.S. government horses that had been taken by a raiding party of Comanches. The Indians liked to take these horses because they made good war ponies.

Seeing something suspicious off in the distance, Captain Carroll brought his men to a halt. He reached for his field glasses and looked down the road.

"Just as I thought," said the captain, handing the field glasses to Sergeant Stance.

"They sure look like army horses to me," said Emanuel. Then he added, "Them Indians is running this way, captain."

Captain Carroll turned to Sergeant Stance and the other soldiers. "When I give the word, we charge," he ordered.

They waited until the Indians got closer. Then, Captain Carroll and his black soldiers charged the band of Comanches. The gunfire from both sides was so loud, you'd have thought the sky was falling. Captain Carroll and his men ran the Comanches into the mountains, and the outnumbered Indians left the horses behind.

Sergeant Stance and a few of the other soldiers rounded up the stolen horses and prepared to take them back to Fort McKavett. But since night had fallen, Captain Carroll ordered his men to set up camp near Kickapoo Springs. They had performed well, and he wanted them to be rested and ready in case the band of Comanches decided to come back for those horses in the morning.

At dawn, the men of the Ninth and Captain Carroll started to head back to the fort with their horses. They were about ten miles outside of Kickapoo Springs when Sergeant Stance began to notice how quiet it was. Not even the birds were singing. He knew from experience that there was going to be trouble. He quickly rode up to the head of the column and asked the captain, "You thinkin' what I thinkin', captain?"

"Yes, I am, sergeant," the captain replied, nodding grimly. "Prepare your men for an attack."

Sergeant Stance rode back and warned his men to be ready. A few moments later, Captain Carroll heard gunfire and spotted a small band of soldiers who had been left to guard another large herd of government horses. A band of twenty Indians, the same group who had been chased off the day before, chased the horses and fired at the small party of soldiers. The soldiers were greatly outnumbered, and Captain Carroll could see that soon the Indians would take the horses and the lives of the soldiers trying to defend them.

Captain Carroll ordered his soldiers to attack. Sergeant Stance, by now a veteran at fighting Indians, immediately led his men straight into the middle of the attacking Indians. Some of the soldiers guarding the horses lay on the ground, wounded; the others were greatly relieved to see that help had arrived.

"Follow me!" shouted Sergeant Stance, as he charged head on into the Comanche gunfire. He fired back, hitting his target with every turn of his pistol. He rode yards ahead of his men, all the while yelling to press the attack.

The Indians fought bravely and fiercely, but they were no match for the well-trained soldiers of the Ninth Cavalry. Again, the Comanches rode back into the hills, leaving the horses behind.

After he was sure that all the Indians had retreated,

Emanuel gathered his men together. Then he rode up to Captain Carroll and saluted.

"That was a fine job you and your men did, sergeant," the captain told Emanuel. "It won't go unnoticed."

"Thank you, sir," Emanuel said proudly. Then he added, "We'd better get those horses back to the fort now, sir."

"Carry on, sergeant," said the captain. He watched as Emanuel rode back to his men and began to supervise the roundup of the horses and care of the wounded. He knew that if it hadn't been for the excellent leadership of Sergeant Stance there would have been many more casualties during the battle.

Captain Henry Carroll didn't forget what he had seen on the battlefield that day. When he returned to Fort McKavett, he recommended Sgt. Emanuel Stance for the Congressional Medal of Honor, our nation's highest honor, which is awarded by Congress to soldiers who have risked their lives in combat above and beyond the call of duty.

On July 24, 1870, Emanuel Stance received his Medal of Honor. He was the first black soldier to receive the medal, and the first of a long line of black men who proved their courage fighting to make this country safe for white settlers.

The Old Cowboy carefully tapped his pipe against the sole of his boot to empty out the tobacco.

"Sundown, that's the story of Emanuel Stance, a little fella with the heart of a lion. He'll always be remembered as one of the bravest fighting men of the Ninth Cavalry, soon to be known as the Buffalo Soldiers. And those soldiers sure had their hands full facing a fierce, clever, and proud Apache Indian named Chief Victorio— the 'Apache Wolf'."

VICTORIO, THE "APACHE WOLF"

The *Old Cowboy glanced over at the African head. The smooth, dark surface shone like velvet in the bright sunshine. The cowboy thought again of the pictures carved on the back of the head. One picture had been of an African warrior standing tall and proud—and free.*

"Sundown, freedom is very special to any person, and when that freedom is threatened, then people will fight to protect their rights. One such person was the Apache chief Victorio.

By 1879, many Indians had been rounded up and moved to reservations that had been mapped out by government officials. Some of the most prime land had been set aside for white settlers, and the Indians were given whatever leftover land remained. According to the treaties, no white man had any right to hunt on Indian land. But some white settlers didn't honor these agreements. They frequently found reasons to trespass on Indian soil to hunt, and often killed animals for profit. The Indians relied heavily on those animals, including the buffalo, for survival.

In August 1879, Victorio and a few Warm Springs Apaches, along with some anxious Mescalero Apaches, rode out of Fort Stanton reservation in New Mexico Territory. They were angry over an incident involving a hunting party made up of a white judge and his lawyer friend, who had trespassed on their reservation. Victorio and his men had been forced to live and hunt on a reservation, when they once had roamed and hunted wherever they pleased. And now even their reservation wasn't off limits to white people if they felt like trespassing whenever they wanted to. Victorio decided it was time to fight instead of live in a white man's world that put boundaries around his people like barbed-wire around cattle to keep them in line.

After Victorio made up his mind to fight, he wasted no time in striking back. His first raid was against a group of sheepherders. Then he made even a bolder move. On September 4, 1879, Victorio, with sixty warriors, attacked a detail of the Ninth Cavalry and got away with a herd of their best horses. It was a lightning strike that left eight troopers of Company F either dead or wounded and minus forty-six of their best mounts. Victorio continued his attacks, killing over nine people in just six days. Colonel Edward Hatch, the commanding officer of the Buffalo Soldiers, put every company of his regiment on the Apache's trail. Their mission: to stop Victorio.

After about sixteen days, the men of the Ninth found Victorio. A detachment led by Lieutenant Colonel Dudley tracked the Apache chief to the canyons of Las Animas Creek in southern New Mexico. The Ninth Cavalry had been led into battle many times by brave and gallant white officers. However, this time they were led by an officer who didn't know much about fighting Indians—especially an Apache as sly as Victorio. The men of the Ninth followed Lieutenant Colonel Dudley into a canyon, but they worried that they were riding straight into trouble.

"If we keep going down into this canyon we gonna get trapped, sergeant," one of the soldiers said.

"That's just like Victorio. His trail is leading us right into an ambush. Look around, all you see is tall rocks and we riding right in the middle with no cover," warned another soldier.

The sergeant nodded. He knew as well as the men did the tricks Indians could pull, like leading soldiers up a false trail and then opening fire on them. He rode up to the front of the column and reined in beside the lieutenant colonel. "Shouldn't we stop and take cover now, sir?" he asked.

"No, sergeant, we move on. We've got him on the run now. He can't be far," said the lieutenant colonel. No sooner had the words left the lieutenant colonel's mouth, than rifle fire rang out through the canyon.

"I told you it was a trap," muttered one of the soldiers, as he and the others quickly dismounted. They grabbed whatever cover they could find and dodged bullets that were ricocheting off rocks in every direction. This was exactly what Victorio wanted. His men were high up in the mountains, firing at the enemy who were pinned down without much cover.

The lieutenant colonel had led his men directly into a trap, but he was lucky that day. Companies C and D happened to be searching nearby and heard the gunfire. They galloped to the scene to join the fight. But all the soldiers could do was to try to defend themselves against Victorio from their awkward position down in the canyon. After fighting all day, Lieutenant Colonel Dudley ordered his men to retreat, leaving five troopers and three scouts dead along with thirty-two horses.

The Ninth Cavalry wasn't accustomed to defeat, and they blamed the disaster in Animas Canyon on their commanding officer. Every man of the two companies felt that a greenhorn like Dudley was unfit to lead Buffalo Soldiers into battle with the crafty Victorio. Furthermore, the men of the Ninth were determined to avenge the deaths of their comrades. But first they needed a proven officer to lead them.

When news of the defeat reached headquarters and Colonel Hatch learned how poorly Lieutenant Colonel Dudley had commanded his troops, he was angry and upset. He had Dudley transferred and sent for Maj. Albert Morrow.

"Major, I've called you here because of the near disaster at Las Animas Creek under Lieutenant Colonel Dudley," said Colonel Hatch. "I want Victorio. He's making a laughing stock of the U. S. Army, and I want him stopped."

"Yes, sir," the major said with a nod. He knew all about Victorio and how he had been outwitting and defeating the men of the Ninth Cavalry. He had trained those black soldiers and fought side by side with them. They deserved better than to be commanded by Lieutenant Colonel Dudley.

"I need you to command the Ninth. You're someone they respect and I know if anybody can catch Victorio, it's you and the men of the Ninth," continued the colonel. "So I'm placing you in command of operations in southern New Mexico. I don't care what it takes or how long it takes. Stop Victorio before he kills more innocent people."

"I understand sir," Major Morrow replied. "My men will

find him and stop him.'' He saluted, turned and left the colonel's office, a pleased expression on his face. He was glad he would be leading the Ninth Cavalry again.

Having their old major back at the command was sweet music to the ears of Ninth Cavalry. They knew the major was as tough as they were and aware of the tricks the Indians could play on soldiers. The next morning, with detachments from B, C, and G Companies of the Ninth and a group of Apache scouts, Major Morrow found Victorio's trail. Soon the soldiers were tailing him as if they were his shadow.

For eleven long days Major Morrow and the Ninth tracked Chief Victorio. Then one of the scouts finally spotted him. He galloped up to Major Morrow and said breathlessly, ''Victorio, Victorio, he only one mile from here, sir!''

''Good, we'll move in now,'' the major said. He moved his men closer to Victorio and got them into position. When they were ready he shouted, ''Charge!''

The word echoed through the mountains and the trumpets blared as the mighty soldiers of the Ninth galloped toward Victorio. They swooped down on the Apache chief and his men like a hawk on a squirrel. Victorio and his men saw the Ninth coming and rode at top speed, guns firing.

Both parties fought from high noon until ten o'clock that evening, September 29, before each side retreated in order to rest. The Ninth Cavalry knew it was in for a tough fight. Victorio was proving to be more than just an average fighter. He was smart and he had total control of his men. And he was fighting to regain the land that was once his—the land the U. S. government had stolen from him and his people. Even though the soldiers' job was to stop Victorio, they couldn't help but respect him for his pride, determination, and cleverness in battle.

The next morning, fighting broke out again between the Apaches and the soldiers. This time, the Ninth had Victorio on the run. For two hours, the soldiers chased him. Finally Major Morrow called off the chase, figuring he'd wait until midnight to track him down again. Then he and his soldiers could attack at dawn. It wasn't a bad plan, but when midnight came, Victorio had outsmarted the U. S. Army again; he had fled into the mountains with his men and vanished.

There were more skirmishes with Victorio and his men after that. And each battle ended with Victorio slipping silently away like a puff of smoke blowing away in the wind. With every successful battle against the army, Victorio's band of warriors grew, and he continued his raids on settlers. As his ranks grew, so did his confidence. No matter what the soldiers did, no matter how close they got, Victorio led them on blind trails to nowhere, and then attacked them. It was becoming clear the cavalry needed help, so Colonel Hatch formed three more battalions. This was one of the largest regiments of troops ever put together. Colonel Hatch hoped that the great numbers of soldiers would finally be able to put an end to the terror caused by Victorio. One of those battalions included the men of the Ninth Cavalry, led by Major Morrow.

Major Morrow left Fort Bayard, New Mexico, in March with Companies H, L, and M of the Ninth Cavalry. This time they all thought they had a good chance at stopping Victorio. Their plan to capture him seemed as solid as a silver dollar. The plan was to surround Victorio in the Hembrillo Canyon near Mexico. Major Morrow's soldiers would come at him from the north, and Captain Henry Carroll's men would attack from the south. This would cut off any chance of an escape. But there was one hitch: each squad had to arrive there at the same time. If one of the squads arrived late, the other squad would have to face Victorio and his men alone. Colonel Hatch's plan relied heavily on the judgment and experience of Major Morrow, Captain Carroll, and the men of the Ninth Cavalry. It was critical that the major be in position to support Captain Carroll by the morning of April 8, otherwise Carroll would find himself stuck in a beehive of fighting Apaches and probably outnumbered. All was going well, until the sergeant rode up to the major with some bad news.

"It's no use sir, the water pump is broke, you can't get much water from it," he reported.

"We're in real trouble now," said the major. They were at Aleman: the only watering hole in that area of Arizona Territory. Morrow's men had been marching all day in the desert heat, and their water supply was nearly empty. He knew they couldn't mount an attack in the morning if his soldiers and their horses were thirsty.

"Okay, sergeant, we'll have to do the best we can. I just hope Carroll can hold on 'til we get there," said the major.

He thought for a moment, then he turned to his second in command. "McClellan," he said, "I want you to take a group of men on a night march to assist Captain Carroll. The rest of us will join you later."

The lieutenant saluted and rode off to gather his men together.

When Captain Carroll and his men arrived at the southern rim of Hembrillo Canyon, they took up position and waited for daybreak.

"You think this plan will work, captain?" asked one of the soldiers.

"I have complete confidence in Major Morrow," replied

the captain. "We've finally got Victorio exactly where we want him. He'll be surrounded."

At dawn the next morning, Victorio and his men began their attack with a round of gunfire. Captain Carroll and his soldiers shot back, but it soon became clear that they were outnumbered. The captain looked around and saw his men being picked off one by one. Where are Major Morrow and his men? he thought desperately. We'll all be killed if he and his men don't get here soon.

Moments later, the captain and his soldiers heard the faint sound of a bugle. The sound grew louder and louder. Both Carroll and Victorio knew the bugle was sounding a cavalry charge. Then Lieutenant McClellan and the men of the Ninth arrived in a cloud of dust, rifles firing, as they dismounted and took cover.

Victorio and his warriors quickly scattered further into the mountains leaving behind eight badly wounded soldiers, including Captain Carroll, and twenty-five dead horses and mules. No one knew for sure how many of Victorio's men had been killed. The Apaches always carried their dead or wounded with them.

"Thank God you got here, lieutenant," said the captain as he was having his wounds dressed. "But what took you so long? And where are Major Morrow and the others?"

"Take it easy now, captain," replied McClellan. "Major Morrow will be here shortly. He'll explain everything."

When Major Morrow and his men did arrive the next morning, they were horrified at the defeat Captain Carroll and his soldiers had suffered. Victorio had once again outfoxed and outsmarted the U. S. Army.

Soon after the battle of Hembrillo Canyon, every army outpost was detailed to capture Victorio. It became clear that Colonel Hatch needed more help, so in March 1880, Col.

Benjamin Grierson, who had trained and formed the all-black Tenth Cavalry, received orders to join the hunt for Victorio.

One way the army felt it could put a dent in Victorio's numbers of recruits was to make sure the Mescalero Apaches stayed unarmed and on their reservation. The Mescaleros made up the majority of Victorio's recruits, and they provided him with supplies, guns, and ammunition. Grierson knew this and watched the Mescaleros closely. He figured it would just be a matter of time before they would try to join Victorio.

One evening, the well-hidden Grierson spotted a band of Mescaleros, some mounted and others on foot, leaving the reservation. Grierson quickly alerted his men, and the chase was on. Shots were fired by the Indians and returned by Grierson's men. The soldiers rounded up a few Mescaleros but over forty escaped.

By now, Victorio was known as the "Apache Wolf." His cunning and ferocity were legendary, and he seemed to be able to appear and disappear at will. It was impossible for officers and soldiers to predict where or when he and his men would attack. But there was one occasion when the Buffalo Soldiers were ready and waiting for him. The man responsible for the soldiers' preparedness was a black sergeant named George Jordan, and because of this and other battles, he received the Medal of Honor.

Sergeant Jordan had over fourteen years of experience fighting Indians and was considered by his superiors to be a capable leader. He had heard about the sly "Apache Wolf" from some of the other soldiers but he had never seen him close up.

On May 14, 1889, at Fort Tularosa, New Mexico, Sergeant Jordan got his chance to see Victorio in all his glory.

That morning the company commander, a captain, called Sergeant Jordan over to him. The captain had assembled a raiding party of soldiers that was packed and ready to ride out into the desert. He shifted in his saddle and barked an order to Jordan. "Sergeant, I want you to take command of the fort. Victorio has been spotted raiding settlers' homesteads, and I'm going after him. But I want you to stay in charge of the men here until I get back."

"Yes, sir," replied the sergeant.

"I'm leaving you twenty-five men," the captain continued. "We shouldn't be gone more than a couple of days."

"All will be secured, sir," Jordan said, saluting.

The captain returned Jordan's salute. Then he and his men rode out to join the other companies to search for the "Apache Wolf."

It was a bright, sunny day. As Sergeant Jordan watched the captain ride off, it occurred to him that this would be a perfect time for Victorio to attack the fort. The weather was good, and Jordan was sure the clever Apache chief would discover that most of the soldiers had left with the captain.

Jordan thought for a minute, then he called his men together, "Private, sound reveille," he ordered. The private blew reveille, and all the troops came front and center, forming two ranks in the middle of the parade ground.

"Men, I've called you together because I have a strong feeling we might get attacked by Victorio and his men today," Jordan told them in a loud, firm voice. "The captain has left me in charge of the fort and I don't want nobody caught off guard. I want every soldier to man his duty station and be on the watch for Indians."

He stepped up to one of the soldiers. "Private, I want that cannon in position on our weak side," ordered Jordan.

"Yes, sergeant," the private answered, saluting.

"All right, men, you have your orders," said Sergeant Jordan.

The soldiers immediately began to take up their positions. Each man knew what he had to do. They all respected the sergeant, and if he thought something was up, they believed him.

Once everything was in place, the men of the Ninth Cavalry stood and waited. After several hours, a soldier said to the man standing next to him, "You think old Sarge might of jumped the gun?"

"Sarge's got fourteen years fightin' Indians. How many you got?" the other soldier snapped back. "Sarge knows what he's doing. You just wait and see."

Just then, the sentinel shouted out, "I see something, Sarge, to the west!"

Jordan rushed over to him and grabbed the field glasses. He saw a band of Indians galloping toward the fort in a cloud of dust. He turned to his men and shouted, "Man your positions!"

Every man was ready within seconds after hearing the command. The cloud of dust got closer, and the soldiers could clearly see the band of Apaches barreling their way. Jordan had been right—Victorio had known that Fort Tularosa would be undermanned. But what Victorio didn't know was that the soldiers were ready for him, and that they were the toughest fighting men in the army.

"Don't fire until I give the word," shouted Sergeant Jordan.

The soldiers waited. Victorio's men got closer, and the sergeant counted over a hundred screaming Apaches riding hard in their direction. All twenty-five of the Buffalo Soldiers knew it was up to them to keep Fort Tularosa in one piece, so every soldier took aim and waited for the signal.

"Fire!" shouted the sergeant, and like a clap of thunder, each rifle went off at the same time. Victorio's men began to fall, but the rest of them kept coming. Some got to the doorway of the fort and tried to break it down, while others rode around the back and tried to climb the wall.

The Indians were everywhere, but the Buffalo Soldiers refused to be overpowered. Hand-to-hand fighting broke out in different parts of the fort, and it was then the Indians knew they were battling soldiers who were well-trained and determined to beat them. As Apaches poured over the top of the fort, they were met with lightning blows from the butts of Winchester rifles or fists as hard as steel.

Sergeant Jordan, one of the best marksmen in the company, was standing at the top of the fort with a line of soldiers. He and his men picked off any Indian that came within thirty feet of the fort.

When the fighting had died down, Jordan looked out into the distance. Coming into view was a lone Indian chief sitting on a beautiful white stallion. Jordan knew that this was Victorio. He saw him stop. Sitting as still as a statue, the "Apache Wolf" raised his arm. Instantly, what remained of his raiding party turned and rode off toward him. Sergeant Jordan and his soldiers watched as Victorio and his men galloped away. The "Apache Wolf" had lost this battle, and many of his men had been killed. All twenty-five soldiers of the Ninth Cavalry had survived with nothing but a few bruises.

Sergeant Jordan showed leadership, courage, and daring in this and other battles with Indians. For his performance in combat above and beyond the call of duty, Jordan was awarded the Medal of Honor at Fort Robinson, Nebraska, in 1890.

After the battle at Fort Tularosa, the walls started to close in on the "Apache Wolf." Every time he fought the soldiers of the Ninth and Tenth Cavalries he lost more and more of his men. One incident struck Victorio an especially heavy blow. Captain Lebo and K Company of the Tenth Cavalry were scouting for Victorio in the Sierra Diablo mountains. They had been on his trail, and as usual, Victorio was one step ahead of them. But this time they didn't give him a chance to cover his tracks. That afternoon, one of the scouts came back with one of the best pieces of news the captain and his soldiers had heard all day.

"Captain, sir," said the excited soldier, as he jumped off his horse. "Victorio, I found his camp."

Captain Lebo ordered his men to mount up, and faster than dust devils, they took off with the private leading the way. When they got there, they couldn't believe their eyes. They had found one of Victorio's largest supply camps. Victorio had posted only a handful of guards to watch the camp, and Captain Lebo's soldiers were able to overpower them easily. The captain and his men captured over twenty-five head of cattle and a great deal of food and ammunition.

Victorio had many of these camps hidden in the mountains, and he used them to resupply his armies. Now they were being discovered and destroyed by the U. S. Army.

Because of the successes of Lebo and others, the army forced Victorio to take more and unnecessary risks.

Col. Benjamin Grierson of the Tenth Cavalry knew that Victorio badly needed water.

In 1880, on one of the hottest days in August, Grierson placed C and G Companies of the Tenth Cavalry under Captain Viele to guard the watering hole at Rattlesnake Canyon. They had gotten a tip that Victorio was on his way there to renew his water supply. The plan was to attack him while he and his men drank and filled their canteens.

"You all know what to do," Viele told his men. "Nobody fires until I give the word. We don't want to scare him off."

The trap was put into place. A handful of soldiers positioned themselves by the water hole, out of sight. Most of the men hid back behind large rocks. The men of the Tenth crouched down and waited in the searing heat for Victorio. Then, one of the scouts looked into his field glasses and spotted something coming through the canyon. Silently, he handed the glasses to Captain Viele, who looked through them carefully.

"It's him," he said with a nod, as he glimpsed the Apache chief on his white stallion. Without taking his eyes off Victorio, he raised his hand slowly. The soldiers tightened their hands on their rifles and waited for the captain to give the first signal. Victorio and his men were still out of rifle range, and Captain Viele wanted them to get just a little closer.

"Come on, Victorio, come on," whispered the captain.

Right in the middle of Rattlesnake Canyon, Victorio brought his men to a sudden stop. His experience told him something wasn't right. Captain Viele realized that Victorio had sensed a trap, and he let his hand fall. Immediately, the soldiers by the water opened fire.

Victorio quickly led his men out of firing range. But he had only seen part of the trap, a handful of soldiers. His need for water that day overcame his thinking. Figuring he was facing just a few soldiers, Victorio turned his men around and charged. As he did, Captain Viele gave the second signal, and Companies H and B swarmed down from all sides, rifles firing lead so hot, it sent fiery sparks right through the sky. Victorio and his men were forced back. They scattered into the ravines and hills without the water they desperately needed.

Colonel Grierson of the Tenth and Colonel Hatch of the Ninth Cavalries were coming closer to stopping the ''Apache Wolf'' once and for all. The colonels and their soldiers pursued him and his men with relentless determination. Victorio's ranks were getting smaller, and he had hardly any supply camps left. Soon he and his men started making raids on wagon trains and settlers again, taking whatever they could get their hands on.

At that time the Mexican government would not allow American soldiers to enter Mexico to arrest outlaws no matter what crime they had committed in this country. Many outlaws took advantage of this situation, including the ''Apache Wolf.'' Victorio would break the law in the United States and run for Mexico, where Grierson and his soldiers could do nothing but stop and watch the Apache chief and his men ride across the border to safety. After a great deal of wrangling between the two countries, Mexico agreed to join forces with the United States to stop the ''Apache Wolf.''

One of the largest and most powerful regiments of soldiers was put together under Col. George Buell and Col. Eugene Carr. They planned to chase Victorio into Mexico and join up with Mexican troops under the command of Col. Joaquin Terrazas. The combined force would overpower Victorio and the American troops would capture him. Colonel Grierson and ten companies of the Buffalo Soldiers were posted along the Rio Grande to make sure Victorio and his men wouldn't come back into Texas.

On a day in October 1880, scouting reports had traced Victorio to the Tres Castillos Mountains in Mexico. Colonels Buell and Carr quickly closed off all possible escape routes. It looked like the long and bloody career of the ''Apache Wolf'' would soon be over.

''Well, colonel, we're finally going to catch that rascal,'' Colonel Carr said to Colonel Buell the evening before they and their soldiers crossed the border into Mexico.

Colonel Buell nodded. ''In the morning, the U. S. Army will close the chapter on the 'Apache Wolf','' he replied. ''We've waited a long time for this moment.''

But early next morning, Colonel Buell was awakened by a voice outside his tent.

''I must speak to Colonel Buell, it is a matter of most importance,'' he heard a Mexican soldier say to his guards.

Colonel Buell stepped out of his tent. ''What's the meaning of this?'' he asked sharply, as the soldier saluted. ''We need to prepare to attack soon.''

''I think you had better read this first, sir,'' the soldier replied.

Colonel Buell read the note and his face turned red with anger. ''This is impossible. We had an agreement,'' the colonel said hotly to the soldier. ''And now your government is backing out!''

''I just delivered this message, sir. I didn't write it,'' replied the soldier, humbly.

The colonel nodded and abruptly dismissed the soldier. Then he strode off in a rage to tell Colonel Carr the news that the Mexican government had changed its mind and decided it didn't want American troops on its soil. Mexican troops had surrounded Victorio, and Colonels Buell and Carr had to withdraw their men back to the American side of the Rio Grande.

The men of the Ninth and Tenth Cavalries and Colonels Grierson, Buell, and Carr stood silently and helplessly across the river and watched as Colonel Terrazas and his troops swooped down on Victorio. They attacked from all sides, and by 9 o'clock the "Apache Wolf," along with the remainder of his faithful followers, lay dead in the dirt at the hands of the Mexican government.

The men of the Ninth and Tenth had chased Victorio all over Texas, Arizona, and New Mexico. They had drained much of the fight out of the "Apache Wolf" by the time the Mexican soldiers got to him. As an enemy, he was hunted like a wild animal; as a man fighting to make his people free to live the way they had before the white man came, he was respected. The Buffalo Soldiers and Victorio and his men shared common ground; they were both fighting for what they believed in. Victorio fought for the freedom of the past, to roam this country like his ancestors, free of reservations; the Buffalo Soldier fought for the freedom of tomorrow, hoping that one day he would be counted as equal to any man.

The Old Cowboy reached over and scratched Sundown thoughtfully behind the ears.

"You know, people fight for their freedom in different ways," he said. "Some people fight to be free to become what they want to be. Henry Flipper, the son of slaves, wanted to go to college and then become a Buffalo Soldier. Well, Sundown, he did that and more. He became the first black man to graduate from the United States Military Academy at West Point and the first black officer in the U. S. Army."

LIEUTENANT
HENRY O. FLIPPER,
THE FIRST BLACK
OFFICER IN
THE U.S. ARMY

"Slavery, Sundown, was one of*
the most wicked ways one man could treat another human being,"
began the Old Cowboy. "There ain't no way of gettin' around it.
No human is born to be a slave just because his or her skin is a
different color. But in America before the end of the Civil War,
especially in the South, African men and women and even their
children were owned by white people.

"Sometimes, if an African man and woman were lucky, a
slaveholder would let them keep their family together. That didn't
happen too often, but it did in the case of Festus Flipper and his
wife. They were able to stay together and raise their son, Henry
Ossian Flipper, who became the first African American to graduate
from the United States Military Academy at West Point.

Henry O. Flipper was born into slavery on March 21, 1856, in Thomasville, Georgia. His father Festus, was a shoemaker and a carriage trimmer. He was owned by a man named Ephraim Ponder. Henry and his mother belonged to Reuben Lucky, a Methodist minister. The Flippers lived near each other, so the family was able to see each other often. But that was soon to change.

"I hear Master Ponder is going to Atlanta. What we gonna do?" said Mrs. Flipper worriedly to her husband. "We be miles apart."

"Now, don't you fret none," her husband said soothingly. "Master Ponder seem like a reasonable man. When I tell him we want to keep our family together, maybe we can work somethin' out."

"Maybe if I go to him, Festus, he might take more kindly to letting us stay together," suggested Mrs. Flipper.

Mrs. Flipper went to Master Ponder and pleaded with him not to break up her family, but Ponder shook his head and said, "I can't just give up Festus like that. He's a valuable slave. The only way I see you all staying together is if your master pays my price." He named a price, and then added in a voice as stiff as a new saddle, "Now that's my last offer."

Both Festus and his wife went to Reverend Lucky, but he said he couldn't come up with the sum of money that Ponder was asking. The only solution the minister could think of was an extremely unusual one, to say the least. The Reverend Lucky sold Mrs. Flipper and Henry to Mr. Ponder, but the money used to purchase them actually came from Festus. Festus had managed to accumulate a sizeable amount of money from his work over the years, and he didn't hesitate for a moment using it to keep his family together.

Under the arrangement, Mr. Ponder was to pay Festus back bit by bit whenever he had money to spare.

Atlanta was very different from Thomasville. Many of the slaves there could read and write. One of these slaves opened a little school in Master Ponder's woodshop, and eight-year-old Henry started his first lessons. At first, Henry struggled like a baby colt taking his first step, but he was eager to learn and nothing could hold him back.

"Look at him, Festus. Our son is still reading by the candlelight. You sure his sight will be alright?" his concerned mother would often whisper to her husband.

"He'll be just fine," Henry's father would reply proudly. "That boy's gonna be somebody. Can't nothing stop him from learning, not even the darkness."

In 1864, the Civil War was slowly coming to an end, but word reached Atlanta that General Sherman and his Union troops were marching to the city. Ephraim Ponder gathered up all his slaves and fled with them to Macon, Georgia. When General Sherman arrived in Atlanta in the late summer of 1864, he ordered the city to be set on fire. Most of Atlanta was burned to the ground. In the spring of 1865, Festus Flipper and his wife and son moved back to Atlanta. They were now free.

When young Henry returned to Atlanta, he didn't have to study in the woodshop of a slaveholder. Instead he went to schools run by the American Missionary Association. He studied hard, and his teachers became impressed by his intelligence and liveliness. As he grew older, he began to think about what he wanted to do when he finished school. He told his parents, "I want to go on to college and then become a military man. I want to be an officer."

"If that's what you want, you've got our support," replied his father.

Henry's mother nodded and smiled in agreement. "We're very proud of you, son," she said.

In 1869 Henry Flipper entered Atlanta University. During his four years in college, Henry's desire to become an officer in the U. S. Army grew stronger. He had heard about the all-black unit the U. S. Army had formed, the Ninth and Tenth Cavalries. Stories about these tough black soldiers had been passed along, and every black person who heard them was filled with pride. More than anything, Henry wanted to ride with the mighty Buffalo Soldiers.

After Henry graduated from Atlanta University, he and his father talked again about Henry's desire to become an officer. They knew that the only place where Henry could get the best military training was the United States Military Academy at West Point. Through the recommendation of Congressman J. C. Freeman, Henry entered West Point in 1873.

Life wasn't easy for African Americans at West Point. They were harassed and treated with suspicion. Two young black men had entered West Point before Henry Flipper, and they didn't finish their training. One of the reasons they didn't graduate was because of the treatment they received by the young white cadets. James W. Smith, the first black man to attend the academy, was booted out because he struck back at a white boy who had been harassing him. Another young black man, Johnson Whittaker, was kicked out of West Point when he was found tied up to his bed with his ears slashed. Unbelievably, he was court-martialed and expelled because the authorities decided that he had slashed his own ears, tied himself up, and accused the white cadets.

Henry Flipper knew that West Point would be hard, but

he was determined to fulfill his boyhood dream of becoming an officer and riding with the Buffalo Soldiers. No matter what happened, he wouldn't let unfriendly white cadets destroy that dream.

During Henry's first year at West Point, some of the white cadets spoke to him, but those that did were snubbed by their friends. Soon, none of the white cadets spoke to him at all. Henry didn't seem to mind. He just worked hard and kept to himself. Even the teachers tried to discourage him. But the more they tried, the harder he would study, and finally Henry O. Flipper rose to the top of his class and graduated with honors on June 14, 1877. Amazingly, on the day Henry graduated, those white cadets who had refused to speak to him came up and shook his hand.

"Any idea where you're going to be assigned?" one of the white cadets asked Henry.

"I hope they give me what I requested," replied Henry. "A commission with the Buffalo Soldiers of the Ninth and Tenth Cavalries."

"I put in for the Seventh Cavalry," the white cadet said. "I want to ride with General George Custer. You've heard of him, haven't you?"

Henry nodded slowly. "Yes I have," he replied. "He'll probably be famous one day." Henry knew all about General Custer. He had heard how the general had refused to take a higher rank when asked to command the all-black Ninth and Tenth Cavalries. He'd also heard that some of those battles with Indians the general claimed as victories were against women, children, and old men, when their braves were away fighting.

Soon after graduating, Henry received his orders. When he read them, his heart started beating louder than the bass drum in the West Point marching band. As second lieuten-

ant, Henry O. Flipper would report to Fort Sill, Indian
Territory, assigned to the Tenth Cavalry. He had realized his
dream at last.

When Henry arrived at Fort Sill, he stepped into the office
of the company commander.

"Lieutenant Henry O. Flipper reporting as ordered, sir,"
said Henry, as he saluted and handed his orders over to the
commander.

"At ease lieutenant," said the commander, returning the
salute. He looked at Henry appraisingly. "So you're the first
of your race to graduate from West Point."

"That's correct, sir," Henry replied firmly.

The commander nodded. "I can assure you lieutenant,
that the men you're going to command here are some of the
best soldiers in this army," he said. "And if you can be half
as good a leader as they are fighters, you will have done
yourself proud. Have I made myself clear, lieutenant?"

"Yes, sir," replied Lieutenant Flipper proudly. Hearing a
white officer praise the Buffalo Soldiers like that pleased
Henry. At West Point, many of the white officers spoke of
black soldiers as cowardly and undependable fighters, even
though they knew that black soldiers had fought bravely in
every major American war. Henry was glad to hear a white
officer speak the truth about the Tenth Cavalry.

Moments after Henry arrived at Fort Sill, it was hit by a
raiding party of Comanches. They galloped into the fort and
made off with a herd of the best cavalry mounts. Soon after
that raid, over 2,000 Comanches came back and held a war
dance around the fort demanding food for their families. For
a young lieutenant fresh out of West Point, it was a dramatic
introduction to the Indians and their anger.

After spending some time at Fort Sill, Henry was transferred to Fort Davis, Texas. There, he was assigned the dangerous task of tracking down the fierce and clever Apache chief Victorio. But no sooner had he arrived at Fort Davis, when he was ordered to move on to Fort Quitman along the Rio Grande. At Fort Quitman his assignment was the same: to stop Victorio.

Late one night, two soldiers came walking into the fort.

"Halt! Who goes there?" shouted the soldier who was on guard duty. He stared at the two men. They were wearing only their underwear.

"Private Baker and Private Johnson," replied Private Baker hoarsely. "We walked over forty miles to get back here."

"Who's your commander?" Private Johnson asked the guard.

"Captain Nolan," he replied.

"Take us to him, quick," said Johnson. The soldier led the men to the captain's headquarters. "This better be important," he muttered, as he knocked on the door.

"It's a matter of life and death," replied Private Johnson.

The door opened. Captain Nolan looked at the three soldiers sleepily. "What's the meaning of this," the captain said crossly. "Do you realize what time it is?" Then he saw the two soldiers standing before him in their underwear. He blinked in disbelief. "Where are your uniforms, soldiers?" he asked.

"We got hit forty miles from here by some of Victorio's men," Private Baker explained. "He's planning something, Captain. He's on the warpath."

Captain Nolan was known for his skill in fighting Indians and for his ability to sometimes think like one. If Victorio was planning to attack, it was only because he was sure he would win. He also knew that Colonel Grierson had only a handful of soldiers of the Tenth at Eagle Springs. Nolan needed to get a dispatch to the colonel quickly to warn him before Victorio got there first.

"Soldier, take these men to sick bay," ordered Captain Nolan. "And then have that new officer, Lieutenant Flipper, report to me immediately."

Lieutenant Flipper was awakened from his sleep by someone pounding on his door. When he answered, he was told to report to Captain Nolan on the double. Henry dressed quickly and hurried over to the captain's tent.

"Lieutenant Flipper reporting as ordered, sir," said a groggy Henry, as he saluted.

"Lieutenant, I want you to gather your wits about you," said Captain Nolan seriously. "The lives of your fellow soldiers and a great commander depend upon it. I have word that Victorio and his men are planning an attack," the captain continued. "I feel strongly that he'll hit Colonel Grierson and a handful of his men at Eagle Springs. Someone has to get to him first with this dispatch. That someone, Lieutenant, is you."

By now Lieutenant Flipper was wide awake. He felt a tingle of excitement race down his spine. "You can count on me, sir," he said evenly.

"Good," replied Captain Nolan, with a nod. "I want you to go over to the stables, and pick out the fastest horse you can find, and be out of here at daybreak. I know you haven't been here long and this assignment is very dangerous, but a dear friend and some of the best fighting men this army has ever seen could be wiped out. You have your orders, lieutenant. Do you have any questions?"

"No, sir, I understand completely," said Lieutenant Flipper, as he saluted again.

"Godspeed, soldier," said the captain, returning the salute.

Henry jogged over to the stables. He knew what kind of horse he wanted, and he hoped he would be able to find him. Back at West Point, Henry had had a reputation as a fine horseman. His daddy had taught him how to handle animals when he was a child. He became especially skilled at communicating with horses.

There must have been over a hundred horses in the corral that night. Henry began to look over each one closely. Then he heard a horse neigh softly behind him. He turned and his face lit up with pleasure. In the stall behind him stood one of the most beautiful midnight-black stallions Henry had ever seen. He carefully approached the animal, all the while talking softly and steadily.

"I've found you, you belong to me, that a boy, come to me, come to me," Henry chanted quietly.

As Henry stepped closer, the stallion tried to move to the right and back away from him, but Henry blocked his path. The stallion tried to move to the left, but again Henry was there. He kept on talking to the stallion gently but firmly. The stallion tried one last time to shake himself out of the spell of Henry's voice by rearing up on his hind legs and whinnying loudly. When he came down on all fours, he snorted and shook his mane. Then he lowered his head. Henry walked back over to him. "That a boy, you get that out of your system," Henry said as he patted the stallion's velvety neck. "You belong to me, now." The mighty stallion stood there quietly while his new master put a bridle on him.

After Henry had saddled up his stallion, he galloped out of the fort toward Eagle Springs. As he rode, all he could think about was getting there before Victorio. He remembered stories from some of the other black soldiers about this Indian chief who they called the "Apache Wolf." He also knew that Victorio was a very dangerous opponent who many times took no prisoners.

Henry rode for two days through the blistering heat, seldom stopping to water his horse. His route took him into hostile Indian territory, where he was spotted twice by unfriendly Apaches—probably a small group of Victorio's men. But each time Henry saw Apaches ahead, he whispered in his black stallion's ear, and the horse galloped even faster, leaving behind a trail of dust and a group of surprised Indians.

"Halt, who goes there?" asked the soldier on guard duty. But Henry galloped past him into the camp. He stopped in front of Colonel Grierson's tent and dismounted quickly. He was exhausted from his long ride, but he managed to stand at attention when Colonel Grierson came out of his tent. Henry saluted and handed the general the dispatch.

"I rode past two groups of Apaches, but I didn't see any sign of Victorio," Henry reported a bit breathlessly.

"At ease, lieutenant" said Colonel Grierson. He read the dispatch, then turned to his aide. "Sergeant, put all your men on alert," Grierson ordered. "Victorio's in the area."

"Yes, sir," replied the excited sergeant. He saluted and hurried off.

"Get some rest, lieutenant," the colonel told Henry. "And then I want you to ride back to Fort Quitman with orders for Captain Nolan. I need him to move his men here for assistance."

After only a few hours' rest, Henry and his stallion headed back to Fort Quitman. Henry was a few miles away from Colonel Grierson's camp when he heard gunfire. He reined in his stallion and looked toward the camp. A band of

Apaches was galloping toward it. Captain Nolan was right, Victorio had planned to attack Grierson and his men. As Henry galloped back across the desolate west Texas Indian country, thoughts of the Tenth Cavalry pinned down at Eagle Springs painted a terrible picture in his mind.

''Run, boy, run,'' Henry whispered in his stallion's ear. The horse seemed to understand his master's words and the urgency behind them. He shot forward so quickly, Henry nearly fell off him.

Henry got back to Fort Quitman in record time. After he had given Colonel Grierson's orders to Captain Nolan, the captain said, ''Good work, lieutenant. Rest up, because I've got one more assignment for you.''

''What's that, sir?'' asked a puzzled Lieutenant Flipper.

''You're going to lead the rest of the Tenth Cavalry to Eagle Springs to assist Colonel Grierson,'' answered Nolan.

For a moment, Henry wasn't sure he had heard the captain correctly. But then he realized it was true. He was going to lead the men of the Tenth. It was a proud moment for Lieutenant Henry Flipper.

''You move out at daybreak,'' the captain said to Henry. ''Is that clear?''

''Quite clear, sir,'' replied Henry. He saluted smartly and left the captain.

At daybreak, Lieutenant Flipper rode out of Fort Quitman leading the men of the Tenth Cavalry. This was his third trip across the wild Texas landscape, but this time he was crossing it with the gallant and brave Buffalo Soldiers. Henry felt honored that he had the chance to lead them.

When the Tenth Cavalry came riding to the rescue with bugles blaring and rifles firing, they were greeted with relief by Colonel Grierson and his soldiers. They had been able to hold off Victorio and his men, but they fought with more determination now that they had more troops to support them. Victorio and his men pulled back and headed for Mexico. The Buffalo Soldiers chased Victorio to the Mexican border where they had to stop. Eventually, Victorio was killed in Mexico by Mexican army troops.

The battle at Eagle Springs was one of many unforgettable battles for Lieutenant Henry Flipper. He led many charges and gained a reputation for being dependable, courageous, and bold. He was also known as an excellent scout. The army later rewarded him for his outstanding service by appointing him post quartermaster at Fort Davis.

As post quartermaster Lieutenant Flipper was in charge of housing, food, water, fuel, clothing, and equipment for the entire fort. This appointment was quite a change for a young officer whose experience and training had been for field command. He worked hard at his new position but his heart was always in the desert with the fighting troops of the Tenth Cavalry.

Another of Henry's jobs was to account for all the monies spent on supplies. Keeping the books in order for the entire fort wasn't as easy for Henry as planning an attack or rescuing fellow soldiers caught in an ambush set by Apaches. Although he worked diligently at his job, he had to admit to himself that he was bored being a bookkeeper. And his boredom caused him to become a little careless with his math.

At that time, a new company commander arrived at Fort Davis. Colonel W. R. Shafter was known for his strictness, and he could be especially hard on young officers. A pretty young white woman, Miss Andrews, had also come to the fort to visit.

After dinner the first evening of her visit, Miss Andrews

chatted with the officers. She introduced herself to Lieutenant Flipper and said, "I understand you know this country very well, lieutenant. Is that right?"

"Yes, I do, Ma'am," Henry replied politely. "I've scouted this territory at least a hundred miles in every direction."

"Well, I just arrived here, and I'd love to go horseback riding. Perhaps if your schedule permits, you can show me the safer places to ride," she said with a smile.

"I'll be happy to ride with you, Ma'am," Henry said. "It can be dangerous around here if you're not familiar with the countryside. You might run into a band of Indians."

For several summer evenings after that, Miss Andrews and Lieutenant Flipper went riding together. They enjoyed each other's company and were becoming good friends. It didn't occur to him that anyone could possibly disapprove of these rides.

Then one day Colonel Shafter ordered Lieutenant Flipper to bring him the books. Henry stood at attention while the colonel studied them. Finally, the colonel looked up at Henry, an angry expression on his face.

"If my calculations are correct, and I'm certain they are," the colonel said coldly, "we are missing a large sum of money. How do you explain all this, lieutenant?"

Lieutenant Flipper took a deep breath. He realized he must have made errors in his math. He thought the colonel was going to give him a tongue-lashing, but what Shafter said next shocked him to the bone.

"As of now, Lieutenant Flipper, I'm bringing a charge of embezzlement of government funds against you," the colonel said.

Lieutenant Flipper was stunned. Why was the colonel bringing a phony embezzlement charge against him? It soon became clear to him that the real reason for the charge was his friendly concern for Miss Andrews. But Henry couldn't believe that the colonel would ruin his military career because he had gone horseback riding with a white woman. He turned to his good friend Colonel Grierson, for help. The colonel couldn't believe the charges either. He was very familiar with Lieutenant Flipper's record and knew him to be a man of honor.

"I want it to go on record, lieutenant, that I don't believe any of these trumped-up charges," the colonel told Henry. "And I will convey that message to the officers at the court-martial. You've got my word on that as an officer and a gentleman."

Colonel Grierson kept his word. At the court-martial he testified on behalf of Lieutenant Henry Flipper. Colonel Shafter tried to prove that Henry had stolen government funds, but Colonel Grierson countered with records that showed how honorable and dependable Lieutenant Flipper had been in carrying out his duties as an officer. After all the facts had been heard, the officers sitting in judgment could not find proof that Lieutenant Flipper was guilty of embezzlement. The charges against him were dropped. But the army wanted to teach Henry a lesson, so they dismissed him from the United States Army for something called, "conduct unbecoming of an officer."

Henry Flipper, a young man whose dream had been to lead the mighty men of the Tenth Cavalry into battle, who stood firm during the difficult years at West Point, who risked his life to rescue his men, and who brought honor and pride to the Buffalo Soldiers, was booted in disgrace out of the army he loved. He tried many times to appeal his case, but the army refused to listen to him. This treatment might have scarred Henry Flipper for life, but he wasn't just an ordinary man. He took the skills he had learned and turned them into a fortune.

When Henry left the army he headed for Mexico and made a great deal of money as a mining engineer. Later, he was hired by William Green, an investor in mining properties, who wanted him to search for the lost mine of Toyopa. Green paid for Henry to travel to Spain to track down clues that would lead to the mine. He was later employed by Albert B. Fall as a consultant to his Sierra Mining Company. In 1919, when Fall became U. S. Secretary of the Interior, he appointed Henry O. Flipper his assistant.

Henry Flipper overcame the many obstacles in his life to achieve the goals he set for himself. Even when times were rough, Henry knew he'd never give up. It was that mixture of pride and determination that made him a success.

The Old Cowboy got up slowly and stretched. "I think it's a good idea for you and me to go for a walk now, Sundown," he said. "Come on, boy, let's get up that hill over there so we can get a good look at the big, beautiful sky."

Sundown raced ahead of the Old Cowboy, but when he reached the hill, he stopped and waited for his master to catch up. They climbed the hill together and sat at the top. The Old Cowboy gazed out onto a landscape covered with trees and meadows.

"Just look at all that land, Sundown," said the Old Cowboy. "It reminds me of a story 'bout a bunch of settlers called 'boomers' that came stampeding into Oklahoma and Kansas back in 1879."

THE BOOMER
REBELLION

The Old Cowboy leaned back against a rock and clasped his hands behind his head. "Sundown, you see, the government had created a whole separate land just for the Cherokee, Creek, and Seminole Indians. This place, which is now the eastern part of Oklahoma, was called Indian Territory. The Indian groups lived in small settlements in it, and were closely watched by the government. But there was a whole lot of vacant land in Indian Territory, too, land owned by the government but without anyone living or working on it. Before long, land-hungry white settlers cast eyes on it and tried to sneak into Indian Territory to build homesteads. But the U. S. Army ran them off 'bout as quick as a rabbit can twitch his nose. But the settlers kept coming, and pretty soon the situation between them and the army got real bad.

The people who "jumped" on government land and started building homes and working the soil were called "boomers" or claim jumpers. According to the law, they had no right to claim government property as their own.

In the spring of 1879, a newspaper article appeared in the Chicago *Times*. The writer of the article was a Cherokee Indian named Col. Elias Boudinot. He wrote about the richness and fruitfulness of the land and insisted that anybody could just go out there and claim it. Suddenly, land-greedy businessmen and families who wanted a farm or homestead decided to settle or grab as much land as they could in the area that is now eastern Oklahoma.

One of these people was a man named Charles Carpender, who gave himself the rank of "colonel" and led a group of boomers through Kansas to the Indian Territory line. "The land is ours," was his battle cry. "We have the right to take as much as we want and nobody can stop us."

By now, President Rutherford B. Hayes had warned all boomers that homesteading on government land would not be tolerated and he would remove them by force if necessary.

Carpender chose to ignore the president's advice. "Follow me," he shouted as he and his followers approached the border. "They can't stop us." But when his band saw Captain Nolan's Buffalo Soldiers patroling the border, they turned back.

The boomers soon found themselves another leader. David Payne was a stubborn man, a former soldier who had ridden with General Sheridan's troops during the Civil War. Colonel Edward Hatch and his Buffalo Soldiers were called in by General Pope to stop Payne.

"Colonel Hatch, I know that you and your men have just spent months chasing after the Apache chief Geronimo," said the general. "I know I told you and your men to get some rest, but as it happens, I'm going to need your assistance right away. The boomer situation is getting out of hand. These people and their leader, David Payne, must be stopped.''

''I understand, sir,'' the colonel replied with a nod. ''My men are pretty worn out, but as always, they'll rise to the occasion. I'll have them ready.''

Once again the mighty soldiers of the Ninth Cavalry were called upon to protect government lands this time from the mostly white boomers. The Buffalo Soldiers had just finished helping the all-white Seventh and Eighth Cavalries catch Geronimo. And now, while the soldiers of the Seventh and Eighth rested, the men of the Ninth and Tenth had to forgo their rest to fight yet another battle. But they were tough and well-trained and continued to serve as best they could.

David Payne's boomers wanted to settle some prime land in the middle of Oklahoma. Payne was clever as a greased pig and sly as a fox in thinking of ways to get his people past patrols. Most of the time, he was quickly caught by the Buffalo Soldiers and sent home. But Payne seemed to get stronger with every try. By the summer of 1881, he had gathered up enough followers to cause some concern to General Pope and Colonel Hatch.

General Pope added D, E, I, and M companies of the Tenth Cavalry to Colonel Hatch's troops. In November 1881, Payne made his third and last try to set up homesteads in Oklahoma. This time he and his boomers faced over six companies of the Ninth and Tenth Cavalries. Again David Payne was turned back, and this time he stayed quiet for several years.

The Buffalo Soldiers usually treated the boomers kindly, sharing their beans and bacon with them, during the journey back to the border of Kansas and the Oklahoma Territory.

"Look at 'em, they just like us," a Buffalo Soldier observed once. "They want somethin' they can't have. It's a shame all this land got to go untouched. Seem to me the government ought to just give them the land and stop all dis fuss."

"Somehow it don't seem fair at all," another soldier put in. "We run the Indians off the land so the government can keep it, and they won't let nobody work it!"

"They ain't givin' up that easy" said a third soldier. "I think we gonna have a fix on our hands if somethin' ain't done real quick."

That third soldier was right. By the spring of 1884, one of David Payne's partners, William Couch, managed to bring over a thousand boomers to the site of Oklahoma City. They started building cabins and plowing the soil. They even built schoolhouses. Soon, a lieutenant arrived at one of the boomer camps with a detachment of soldiers. He found William Couch's father plowing the soil.

"Hey, mister!" said the lieutenant sharply. "You know this is government property. There will be no more plowing. Stop now, or I'll have to place you under arrest!"

Couch glared up at the lieutenant. "This is God's land, not yours," he said precisely. "I have a right to work this land, just like He intended. Now get off my property!" He turned and went back to his plowing.

The lieutenant dismounted and strode up to Couch. "I'm placing you under arrest," he said, grasping the old man's arm firmly. "You'll have to come with me."

"Oh, no you don't! Get your hands off me," shouted Couch as he struggled to break free from the officer's grip.

"Tie him up and put him in the wagon, sergeant," ordered the lieutenant.

"You ain't seen the last of us yet!" yelled the old man, as the wagon pulled away.

The lieutenant had been angered by the old man's defiant behavior, and he became determined to arrest more boomers that day.

"Sergeant, we're heading over to the main camp," snapped the lieutenant. "Prepare your men to be ready for anything, and I mean anything. These boomers are crazy to think they can defy the U. S. Army. I'll show them who runs things out here."

When the lieutenant arrived at the main campsite, he arrested nine more boomers, including a man named J. D. Odell. When Odell saw what the lieutenant and his soldiers had done to Couch, he became very angry.

"You can't treat a man like an animal," Odell said hotly to the lieutenant. "We got rights too."

"Shut up and get in the wagon, mister," shouted the lieutenant.

"Not on your life," Odell shot back. "You have no right to treat us this way. You untie Mr. Couch this minute!"

The lieutenant said impatiently, "You either come peacefully or we'll take you by force."

"If you want me, you got to take me," said J. D. Odell, backing up slowly.

"Sergeant, arrest him now!" ordered the lieutenant.

Odell was tall, lean, and muscular, and he looked like he could handle himself in a fight. But he wasn't as fast or as strong as the two Buffalo Soldiers. They grabbed Odell and tied his hands behind his back before he knew what had happened.

That night, as the Buffalo Soldiers sat around the campsite, many of them voiced mixed feelings about what they had to do to the boomers.

"Sarge, I think we goin' have some trouble in the mornin'," one soldier, an older man said. "These people seem some kind upset 'bout all these goings on."

"I gets the same feeling, private," the sergeant replied. "It's more of them than us, and if they gets itchy, we might be in a real fix."

"I don't know, Sarge," another soldier put in. "It just seem kind of funny. Why can't they work the land? We took it from the Indians and the land's just a-laying there. These people don't mean no harm."

"Yeh, Sarge," said a third soldier. "When I first came out here and join this here outfit, I sees all this land, and I's start to thinking maybe I can get me a piece of it and start me a little farm or something."

"Now you hush yo' mouth boy," the older soldier said. "You thinkin' like a white man. They ain't goin' give you nothing but a hard road to hoe. All this land is fa the white man. All he want you to do is watch over it fa him. Even if it mean we got to kill Indians, or even his own people, he want this here land all fa hisself, not the colored man."

"De Lord didn't make dis land fa no one man to have all to hisself," the third soldier insisted.

"When I get out of the army, I'm going back to Atlanta," a new young recruit said. "You men can have all this fighting and fussing over land. After I finish school, I plan to be a doctor anyway. I'm sick of fighting Indians and boomers. It's not my idea of making a living."

"You men better get some shut-eye," warned the sergeant. "No tellin' what we goin' wake up to in the morning." He yawned, stood up, and headed into his tent.

The next morning, the lieutenant ordered his men to load the prisoners in the wagon.

"I told you I ain't goin' in that wagon, so get!" said J. D.

Odell, stubbornly as he twisted in the grasp of the Buffalo Soldiers.

The lieutenant sighed inwardly with frustration. He was getting fed up with the boomers, and he had had enough of J.D. Odell, "Tie him to the wagon," the lieutenant shouted to his sergeant.

"Now Mr. Odell," the lieutenant said once the tall man had been tied to the wagon, "You can either walk to Fort Reno or you can be dragged. I really don't care." He mounted his horse and shouted, "Move out!"

The wagon started forward, and J. D. Odell followed alongside it, cursing all the way to Fort Reno.

The lieutenant wasn't finished with this group of boomers yet. There were over a thousand of them, and they all were as stubborn as a trainload of mules. This time, the lieutenant came back to the camp with a troop of more than twenty-five fresh Buffalo Soldiers and six or more Indian scouts to arrest a group that was building a schoolhouse.

"You men know why we're here," the lieutenant said to the boomers wearily. "You can either come peacefully, or my men will force you into this wagon."

"We ain't goin' nowhere!" shouted one of the boomers. "This land don't belong to nobody. We got our rights!"

By this time, the lieutenant's patience had worn as thin as a hair trigger on a Colt .45. "Take 'em!" he shouted to his men. The Buffalo Soldiers rushed forward and so did the boomers. They began to fight each other with their fists.

At that point, the lieutenant lost his self-control. "*Fire!*" he screamed. "Shoot these varmints. You hear me, I gave an order. *Fire!*"

He gave the order again, but the sergeant who had been in tight situations like this before, did not obey it.

"Sergeant, I said, *Fire!*" the lieutenant screamed again.

The sergeant knew his military career was on the line for not obeying a direct order, but he also knew that if he gave the order to open fire on a group of white farmers he and his men would suffer even greater dangers. And he wanted to avoid a bloodbath.

"Take it easy, sir," the sergeant said calmly and coolly. "We got everything under control here. It's alright."

The lieutenant quickly saw his mistake in giving that order, and he told his soldiers to disregard it. The boomers also realized the army was willing to use force on them. Had it not been for the sober thinking of one black sergeant, all of them might have been killed. These boomers surrendered quietly and allowed themselves to be taken under arrest to Fort Reno.

But other boomers had refused to give up. David Payne had been arrested and sent home, but in June 1884, he gathered over 1,500 boomer homesteaders together. He addressed them as they were about to cross the border into Oklahoma Territory.

"Are we determined to plant, build, and provide for our children on the land God created for us?" shouted David Payne.

"Yes!" the homesteaders chorused in reply.

"Come on, then!" Payne shouted. He turned his horse around and started across the border. The boomers in their wagons followed him.

These boomers settled in Rock Falls, Oklahoma. This time, they were prepared to fight the soldiers. Payne sent for Colonel Hatch and showed him his army of boomers.

"I'm warning you, colonel," Payne said to Hatch. "You bring them soldiers out here, there's going to be bloodshed. We are willing to die if we have to."

"This is highly irregular, Mr. Payne, and you know it!"

the colonel replied angrily. "You're placing innocent lives at risk. This is government property!"

"It seems to me, colonel, it's the lives of your boys that're at risk," Payne replied with a cocky smile. He motioned toward the huge mass of men. "Look around you. There're more of us than there are of you."

Colonel Hatch stared at Payne's army. It was true; he and his small detachment of soldiers would be outnumbered by them in a battle. He politely said good-bye to Payne and rode back to the fort. There, he sent a telegraph message to General Pope explaining the situation and asking for reinforcements. The message Hatch received from the general ordered him to "remove the boomers at any cost."

On August 5, Colonel Hatch rode out to Rock Falls to pay another visit to David Payne. This time he was accompanied by Captain Moore and L and M companies of the Buffalo Soldiers.

"Bring me Mr. Payne," Colonel Hatch said to one of Payne's lieutenants who was guarding the camp. The man, taken aback by the sight of so many soldiers hurried off.

Moments later, Payne appeared. When he saw the huge detachment of soldiers, he began to feel less sure of himself.

"You have until sundown to vacate these premises, Mr. Payne, or all of your people will be driven off, I promise you," said a very serious Colonel Hatch.

Payne looked around to see how much armed support he had. He saw to his surprise that many of his people had started to pack up their belongings. He whirled around and faced Colonel Hatch. "You're bluffing," he said desperately. "You wouldn't dare fire on us!" He watched in disbelief as his people packed up their wagons and began to move out of the camp. "He's bluffing. It's only a bluff!" he shouted frantically, as loaded-up wagons of homesteaders rode past him, almost knocking him down. Finally, only 250 boomers were left in the camp. And they soon surrendered to Colonel Hatch without a struggle.

"Alright, men, you have your orders," said Colonel Hatch after every boomer had left the camp. "Burn down every building and cabin in sight!"

It wasn't a very pleasant order to carry out, but the Buffalo Soldiers had to obey it. Every building and cabin in Rock Falls was burned to the ground. It was rumored that David Payne died under mysterious circumstances shortly after that incident, but the boomer rebellion didn't die with him. His trusted friend William Couch took up the fight again.

On a cold December day in 1884, William Couch led over three hundred boomers into Stillwater Creek in Indian Territory. They had started to set up camps when Lieutenant Day and thirty soldiers of the Ninth Cavalry rode out to remove them.

"My orders are to evict you from this land," Lieutenant Day said to William Couch. "Now, have your people load their wagons and move out!"

"We ain't moving, and you ain't got enough men to make us move!" Couch shouted defiantly.

The lieutenant knew he was right. He was badly outnumbered, and if a battle started, he could place himself and his men in serious danger. "You know you'll have to go sooner or later," said the lieutenant.

"It's gonna be a lot later for *you*, if you don't get out of here," Couch replied angrily. "I ain't forgot how y'all treated my daddy!"

Lieutenant Day realized this was one battle he couldn't win, so he and his men carefully pulled out and rode back to the fort.

Lieutenant Day immediately telegraphed Colonel Hatch and filled him in on the problem "They outnumber us ten to one," said Day's message. "I fear some kind of major confrontation will occur unless we suppress this rebellion. I urgently request reinforcements immediately or I fear many lives will be lost." Colonel Hatch quickly answered the lieutenant's telegram, and by January 24, seven companies of the all-black Ninth Cavalry were mounted up and ready under the command of veteran officers.

Captain Carroll, one of the most experienced officers, was selected to ride out to the boomer campsite and speak to Couch. The boomer leader must have gotten word that the captain was coming, because he was waiting for Carroll when he rode up.

"Well, well, you boys must be getting a little nervous, if they sent out a man like you," Couch said sneeringly. "I've heard of the great Captain Carroll and his black Indian fighters. Well, we ain't Indians and we ain't goin nowhere!"

"You people just don't know when you're beaten," Captain Carroll said firmly. "You can't win this so-called battle with the U. S. government. You can either surrender now or risk the consequences."

Couch shook his head stubbornly. "We're tired of running, captain," he said. "We got just as much right to this land as you. What right did you have to take it from the Indians? Now you come out here and say, can't nobody else have the land. This land is ours just like it's yours and anybody else's who wants to claim it. We got rights captain," Couch added fiercely. "And I'm here to tell you we'll fight to the death if we have to."

"Then it's my understanding that you and your people are not going to obey this order to surrender?" asked Carroll flatly.

"You just about figured it out, captain. We ain't goin' no place!" said Couch.

When Captain Carroll returned to the fort, he sent word to Colonel Hatch that the boomers at Stillwater Creek were going to put up a fight if they had to. Colonel Hatch arrived at the fort to talk over the problem with Captain Carroll.

"Couch is trying to force us into a battle, I'm certain of it," said Colonel Hatch angrily. "This is the last straw." He thought for a moment, then he said, "Look, captain, I've got an idea. We'll wait them out."

"Wait them out, sir? They've got food and supplies; a siege could take forever," Carroll replied in a puzzled voice.

"Not if we cut off all food and supply lines into their camp," explained Hatch. "I'll bet my best riding pony that in a few days their empty bellies will tell them it's time to go, and even William Couch won't be able to stop them!"

On January 25, 1885, a morning so cold you could shake hands with your own breath, the siege of Stillwater Creek began. Colonel Hatch surrounded the boomer camp with Buffalo Soldiers. All supplies headed for the camp were confiscated by the soldiers. After the third day, Hatch and the Buffalo Soldiers started seeing signs of weakness in the camp.

"Look a there, private," one of the soldiers said pointing toward the camp. "I think one of them boomers is starting to pull out. Sarge, I see a couple more wagons moving out," shouted another soldier a few hours later.

Hatch's plan had worked. After five days of freezing cold, with no food or supplies, William Couch realized he had been defeated without a bullet being fired. He led his men back to Arkansas City, Kansas.

That was the last time anybody heard from William Couch and his boomers. After the siege at Stillwater Creek, little groups tried to settle in Indian Territory, but they were quickly overcome by the Buffalo Soldiers and sent on their way. Soon Colonel Hatch, Captain Carroll, and their proud Buffalo Soldiers could ride for miles and miles and not see one boomer homestead anywhere.

By June 1885, Colonel Hatch and the Buffalo Soldiers had driven the last boomers out of the Indian Territory. Again it was a job they had to do, a job they got no official thanks for. Things were starting to quiet down a bit in the West. The Indians were pretty much where the U. S. government wanted them, on reservations. The West was much safer now, and more and more white Cavalry units started pouring into what was once the land of the Osage, the Comanche, the Apache, and other Indian groups.

The men of the Ninth and Tenth Cavalries were split up, many going to forts all around the West. Several Buffalo Soldiers sat together soon after they had received their orders and talked about their years with that special cavalry.

"Where you headed Sarge?" asked one soldier.

"Looks like I be goin' to Fort McKinney in Wyoming," replied the sergeant. "What about you?"

"My orders say Fort Robinson, Nebraska," replied the soldier.

"Hey, Sarge, since they splittin' all of us up, you think we can finally get some rest?" said another soldier. "Everytime I turn around, we running off to save somebody."

"They wouldn't be sendin' us off like this unless things must be gettin mighty quiet," agreed the sergeant.

"You think history goin' remember all we did Sarge?" the first soldier asked. "I mean, fighting Victorio, Geronimo, and all them white folks we had to run off the land?"

"I can't see why not," the sergeant replied. "We sho' did it all. I'm the oldest of y'all, and when I joined up I heard about a little short black soldier named Emanuel Stance. Boy, now he was somethin else! He rode straight into gunfire chasing after Indians and not a single bullet touched him. He made every black soldier proud. We all wanted to be just like him. That was nearly twenty years ago. By the time we fought Victorio, we was called the Buffalo Soldiers."

"Is it true, Sarge, the Indians named us Buffalo Soldiers?" asked a young recruit.

"Sure as shootin' they did, son," said the sergeant. "See, when Indians first saw us black soldiers, they didn't know what to think. They was used to fightin' white men."

"I remember my first fight with an Indian," the sergeant continued. "He tried to see if my skin color was some kind of paint that would rub off. But it wasn't long before they saw we was the bravest bunch of soldiers they ever fought. See, when you eye to eye with an Indian and he looks at you, he can see if you a man or a coward. When he had to fight a black soldier, he knew he was fightin' a real man, not no coward. Since our hair feel and look like hair on the buffalo, that's what he called us."

"Wait a minute. The Indians called us Buffalo Soldiers cause our hair is nappy like a buffalo? That ain't nothin'!" said the young recruit scornfully.

The sergeant grabbed the young soldier by the shoulders so hard his cap shifted on his head. "I don't ever want to hear you say that ain't nothin' again, you hear me soldier!" snapped the sergeant.

"The Indian respects the buffalo more than anything. The buffalo give him food to eat and clothes to keep him warm when it be cold. When he calls us Buffalo Soldiers, it ain't cause our hair is nappy, it's 'cause he respects us as fighters and men. You got that, boy?"

"Yes, sir, I mean, Sarge," said the pretty shaken-up young recruit.

The men of the Ninth and Tenth Cavalries finally got the long rest they were promised. They had ridden thousands of miles all over the West, serving their country and doing their duty year after year. White officers like Hatch, Carroll, Cooney, Grierson, and Dodge no longer led their mighty Buffalo Soldiers into battle. Buffalo Soldiers like Emanuel Stance, George Jordon, "Big" Henry Johnson, and Lt. Henry O. Flipper were names that filled the night air when young black recruits listened to old-timers tell the stories of their adventures as Buffalo Soldiers. Time had changed the West, and more and more white settlers moved in.

By 1889, when Colonel Edward Hatch died at Fort Robinson, Nebraska, the Buffalo Soldiers had been reorganized to serve light garrison duty at the forts they had been assigned to. It was a new day for the black soldier, and it must have been tough for them at first getting used to all that quiet, with no officers ordering them to rescue a wagon train of settlers or put down an Indian uprising somewhere. The Buffalo Soldiers wondered if they would ever be called upon to fight again.

The sun was starting to sink lower in the sky. The Old Cowboy knew that he and Sundown ought to be heading back down the hill to the campsite, but he had one more story to tell.

"Sundown, stop chasing that rabbit," said the Old Cowboy. "Come over here to me. I want to tell you about the next time the Buffalo Soldiers had to fight for their country. That's right, their rest was over. They were about to go into action at San Juan Hill during the Spanish-American War."

THE BATTLE OF
SAN JUAN HILL

Sundown barked at the jackrabbit *a few times just to show him that he could have caught him if he really wanted to. Then he trotted over to the Old Cowboy and sat down next to him.*

"Sundown, in 1898, the U. S. battleship Maine *was blown up in Havana harbor in Cuba. The United States blamed Spain and declared war on that country. Some of the soldiers sent to fight the Spanish army in Cuba were the men of the Ninth and Tenth Cavalries, the Buffalo Soldiers. They took their Indian fightin' skills out of the Old West into Cuba, and it was there they fought the battle of San Juan Hill.*

''I heard we might be going to that Cuba place,'' said a Buffalo Soldier.

"I hears the same thing," another soldier replied. "We s'posed to liberate them from the Spanish."

"Like we liberated the Indian from his land," said a third sarcastically.

"You know what I think," he added "I think we ought to stay right here and liberate our self!"

"You know why the government is sendin' us, don't you," the second soldier said. "We s'posed to have some kind of immunity to some kind of sickness over there that the white man don't have."

"Naw, dat ain't it," an older soldier said. "We 'bout the best darn trained soldiers dis here army got. If'en they want to win dis here war in a hurry, dey betta send us!"

As far-fetched as it may sound, the U. S. Army actually *did* think that black soldiers, because they had worked so long and hard in hot weather, could stand the heat in Cuba and somehow not come down with the disease called yellow fever, transmitted by mosquito bites. So the Ninth and Tenth Cavalries and Twenty-fourth and Twenty-fifth Infantry were called to duty once more, this time to protect the rights of a group of people in another country.

The Buffalo Soldiers weren't the only U. S. soldiers to go. There were also two white battalions of the First Volunteer Cavalry, better known as the Rough Riders. One of the officers, who resigned his post as Assistant Secretary of the Navy to join the liberation of the Cubans from Spanish rule, was a future U. S. president, Theodore Roosevelt.

"Are you crazy?" said one of Roosevelt's aides. "You're going to resign as assistant to the Secretary of the Navy to stomp around in the jungles of Cuba?"

"You bet I am," Roosevelt replied with a huge grin. "This is an opportunity that I can't afford to pass up. Besides, this little scuffle will be over in a blink, and when the dust settles, I want the American people to remember it was 'Teddy' Roosevelt and his 'Rough Riders' who liberated those people.''

''But you don't have any military experience, you could get killed,'' insisted the aide.

''With all the military help I'll have, I won't get touched. I'll be back before you know it,'' said Roosevelt, as he walked out of his office.

The Ninth and Tenth Cavalries and Teddy Roosevelt and the Rough Riders were all sailing to Cuba together to liberate the Cubans. But for the Buffalo Soldiers on board ship, it was a long and miserable trip.

''Why do we have to stay down here below decks!'' shouted one soldier to another. ''Ain't our blood the same color as white folks?''

''It ain't right, sergeant.''

''We got to die just like them so-called 'Rough Riders' up on top deck. We down here in the middle of summer wearin' woolens. It just ain't right!''

''I done fought in twenty Indian wars, pulled eight arrows from my body, fought against Victorio and caught Geronimo,'' said one old-timer. ''How many battles them Rough Riders been in!''

''I hear ain't none of 'em been in one battle,'' said another angry Buffalo Soldier.

These Buffalo Soldiers had good reason to be upset. They weren't allowed to mingle on the top deck with the white soldiers. The only time they could leave the ship was to bathe and march for the townfolks. Roosevelt's Rough Riders could go off ship and do whatever they pleased, while the men of the Ninth and Tenth Cavalries, like prisoners, could only look out of the portholes until they reached Cuba.

On June 23, 1898, the angry but well-trained Buffalo Soldiers landed in Cuba ready to fight. Their first target was Las Guasimas. Roosevelt and his Rough Riders got there first and ran into heavy gunfire. One of the reasons he became pinned down by the enemy was his lack of military experience.

"I told him to wait," said an angry Capt. "Black" Jack Pershing, a white officer who had led the Tenth Cavalry for over ten years. He quickly commanded the Buffalo Soldiers to charge and they did. They got there just in time to keep Roosevelt and his Rough Riders from suffering heavy losses. The Buffalo Soldiers knocked out those Spanish rifles that were raining lead on Roosevelt's men and when all the shooting was over, the Spaniards gave up.

Roosevelt's Rough Riders had hardly any military experience. They were mainly a group of old cowboys, college football players, and soldiers of fortune. And they were all led by a man who had no military experience at all.

Another reason why the Rough Riders ran into problems was because they didn't have automatic repeating rifles like the Spanish. When they ran into gunfire, their single-shot rifles were no match for the Spanish soldiers' guns. It was also rumored that the mules that had been carrying the Rough Riders' machine guns had gotten lost or couldn't be found. Either way, if the Buffalo Soldiers hadn't been there with their repeating rifles and charged those Spanish soldiers, it's likely that the Rough Riders would have all been killed.

Another incident at Las Guasimas involved Pvt. Augustus Wally of the Ninth Cavalry. As he charged the stronghold at Las Guasimas, he heard a soldier cry, "I'm hit! I'm hit!" Wally looked to his left and saw that Major Bell, one of his white officers, had been hit in the shoulder and leg.

"Stay down, I'm coming," shouted Wally as bullets flew over his head. As a private fighting Apaches in New Mexico in 1881, Wally had rescued another man who was pinned down under heavy gunfire. That time, he was awarded a Medal of Honor for his actions.

Crawling on his belly, Wally knew that the only way he could get to the major in a hurry was to make a run for it. He stood up and took off, dodging bullets and firing his repeating rifle as he ran. Private Wally made it over to the wounded major and carried him to safety.

The battle of Las Guasimas was over pretty quickly. After about an hour and a half, the Spanish gave up. But the war wasn't over. The next battle between the Spanish and U. S. armies took place at El Caney, a small village. El Caney was protected by two hills. The Spanish army hoped that they could win this battle by holding those hills, which were called Kettle and San Juan.

"Them Spaniards gotta put up a better fight than that if they gonna win this thing," said one Buffalo Soldier the evening before the battle.

"It ain't over yet, private." warned an old-timer.

"I hear we got to take El Caney in de mornin, den de hill after dat."

"Which hill?" asked a young recruit.

"We take Kettle, then we help those Rough Riders over on San Juan," answered another soldier.

"We supposed to get some help from the Twelfth Infantry tomorrow," said the old-timer.

"When they gonna help us, they ain't helped us yet!" remarked another soldier.

That Buffalo Soldier had a point. When most history books mention that battle at El Caney, they don't really report the facts correctly. The way most white historians wrote it, the all-white Twelfth Infantry made the charge all alone with just a little help from the all-black Twenty-fifth Infantry. But the truth was that the men of the Twenty-fifth Infantry fought the battle all by themselves. The Twelfth didn't arrive until the fighting was nearly over. One Buffalo Soldier, Pvt. T. C. Butler of the Twenty-fifth, was about to take the Spanish flag he and his fellow soldiers had captured back to his regiment, when a white officer ordered him to turn the flag over to him. Private Butler stared at the white officer, then ripped a piece of that flag off and handed the rest to the officer. He later explained his behavior to his Colonel in a report that told what had really happened at El Caney.

While this incident was taking place at the outpost in El Caney, other black troops were fighting up Kettle Hill. The Rough Riders, commanded by Theodore Roosevelt, were fighting on San Juan Hill.

"Did you hear what I just heard?" shouted one Buffalo Soldier over enemy gunfire to another. They were fighting on Kettle Hill.

"You betta keep you head down boy, lessen you want it shot off. What'd you hear?" replied the other soldier.

"We got orders to help the Rough Riders again" said the first soldier.

"We got mo' than we can handle right here," the second soldier replied, shaking his head.

The men of the Ninth and Tenth fought the Spanish army hard that day as they charged up Kettle Hill. This battle wasn't as easy as the one at Las Guasimas because the Spanish had the advantage of being able to shoot down at the U.S. troops from high up on the hill. But like Victorio, Geronimo, and the many other Indians that had ever fought a Buffalo Soldier, the Spanish soon learned a tough lesson: a

Buffalo Soldier will never give up until the job is done.

"Charge," was the cry officer Samuel Sumner shouted to his cavalry units as the infantry moved on both flanks of the hill. As the cavalry units tried to move forward, the Spanish gunfire stopped them dead in their tracks. By now a lot of confusion had taken place, and some white soldiers got separated from their units and found themselves fighting alongside black soldiers. The Spanish fought long and hard, but they were no match for the hound-dog tough and sharp-shooting Buffalo Soldiers who soon took Kettle Hill.

Meanwhile, the Spanish had pinned down Theodore Roosevelt and his Rough Riders at San Juan Hill.

"Did you send for reinforcement like I ordered?" Roosevelt shouted to his sergeant.

"Yes, sir, I did, but the Ninth and Tenth ran into heavy resistance over at Kettle Hill," replied the sergeant.

"We're under heavy resistance right here, sergeant," said Roosevelt. "If we don't get some help fast, we'll be wiped out."

Roosevelt's lack of military experience showed itself. He had rushed his men into a hillside full of bushes, tangled vines, and barbed wire. The Spanish military commanders knew that climbing San Juan Hill was going to be tough going for the U. S. troops. They hid their best sharpshooters in the undergrowth to pick off the Rough Riders.

The Ninth and Tenth Cavalries were ordered over to San Juan Hill to help Roosevelt and the Rough Riders. They were led by Maj. Charles Young, the third black graduate from West Point. When the Buffalo Soldiers arrived at San Juan Hill with machine guns blasting, they were met by a relieved Theodore Roosevelt. He knew he would win the battle of San Juan Hill with the Buffalo Soldiers at his side.

The Buffalo Soldiers charged up the hill. Even the old

white cowboys and soldiers of fortune, who made up a large part of Roosevelt's Rough Riders, found new spirit and courage to fight as they watched those black soldiers advance and not retreat like some of them had done. The Buffalo Soldiers moved quickly up San Juan Hill and rooted out most of the sharpshooters from that underbrush. They kept climbing up the hill, all the while pouring rapid fire into the enemy.

But the Spanish refused to give up San Juan Hill without a fight. As the Ninth, Tenth, and Roosevelt's men got close, the Spanish opened up with firepower that surprised even the Buffalo Soldiers. They were sent digging into the sand like a prairie dog dodging a buffalo stampede, grabbing whatever cover they could find.

"We've got them on the run, don't hold back, forward men!" shouted Colonel Baldwin to his soldiers pressing them to attack. He had no sooner shouted these words when a bullet ripped through his shoulder, knocking him off his horse. Sergeant Baker of the Ninth looked over just as the colonel's horse fell down. Under a hail of gunfire, he ran over to aid the colonel.

"No, sergeant, go back and rally the men, I'm alright," whispered the colonel.

"You sure, colonel?" asked the sergeant.

"Yes. Now go back, that's an order!" said the colonel. When Baker got back to his unit, they were already pounding the enemy with gunfire and had moved farther up the hill. He had to hurry to catch up to them.

The enemy was starting to show signs of weakening. By the time the Ninth, Tenth, and the Rough Riders had made it halfway up San Juan Hill, they were in control of the battle. They moved up the hill easily until finally, by late afternoon on July 1, the men of the Ninth, Tenth, and the

Rough Riders had totally defeated the Spanish army at El Caney, Kettle Hill, and San Juan Hill. When Roosevelt and his Rough Riders rode up to the high point of San Juan Hill, they were surprised to see that the men of the Tenth Cavalry were already there.

This war only lasted ten weeks, but it left a mark on history that will never be forgotten. One white corporal said, "If it hadn't been for those black soldiers, we all would have been wiped out." Even Theodore Roosevelt said, "I don't think any Rough Rider will forget the ties that bind us to the Ninth and Tenth Cavalries." He also said, "These men can drink from our canteens anyday." But when he got back to the United States, he changed his tune.

A few months after he returned home, Roosevelt was talking to some newspaper reporters about the role of the black soldier in Cuba. Roosevelt owed his life to the timely arrival of the Ninth and Tenth Cavalries, and he should have had many kind words to say about those fighting black men. But he didn't.

"So how did the all-black units perform in battle, Mr. Roosevelt?" asked one reporter.

"I'm glad you asked that question because I'm sorry to say, I found them very dependent on their white officers," Roosevelt replied. "In fact, on more than one occasion in battle, they would get uneasy and start to drift to the rear. There were times I had to draw my revolver and use it to prevent them from running."

Roosevelt had been elected governor of New York with his eye on becoming president, so perhaps he thought that lying about what really happened over in Cuba was what the all-white voters wanted to hear. No one knows what Rough Riders thought when they read Roosevelt's account of the way the Buffalo Soldiers acted in battle, especially the men who had shown how glad they were to see those black faces come riding to their rescue after they had been led into a snag on San Juan Hill by Roosevelt. And what did a Buffalo Soldier think after seeing Roosevelt make such a claim?

Two days after Theodore Roosevelt became governor of New York, some of the same black soldiers that fought over in Cuba were chased out of Wilmington, North Carolina, like slaves running from bloodhounds, by angry mobs of white people who felt black men held too many official jobs.

The black soldier got little respect all during the settling of this country and during the times he fought in other countries. It was like getting invited to the party, but never being asked to dance. He was always called to serve and to die, but never asked to take part in America.

"Well, Sundown," said the Old Cowboy, "we better head down this hill back to our campsite and get some grub. And I want to take another look at that African head before it gets dark. Tomorrow's another day. Maybe things will get better for the black soldier and black people. All I know is, we can't give up. Like the Buffalo Soldiers, we got a job to do, and we can't rest 'til it's done. Come on, boy!"

BIBLIOGRAPHY

Bonner, T. D. *The Life and Adventures of James P. Beckwourth.* New York: Arno Press, 1969.

Cashin, Herschel V. *Under Fire with the Tenth U. S. Cavalry.* New York: Arno Press, 1969.

Downey, Fairfax. *The Buffalo Soldiers in the Indian Wars.* New York: McGraw Hill, 1969.

Durham, Philip and Jones, Everett L. *The Adventures of the Negro Cowboys.* New York: Dodd Mead, 1960.

Durham, Philip and Jones, Everett L. *The Negro Cowboys.* New York: Dodd Mead, 1965.

Glass, Edward L. N. *History of the Tenth Cavalry, 1866–1921.* Tuscon: University of Arizona Press, 1921.

Goode, Kenneth G. *California's Black Pioneers.* Santa Barbara, Calif.: McNally & Loftin, 1974.

Katz, William Loren. *Black Indians, a Hidden Heritage.* Seattle, Wash.: Ethrac Publications, 1986.

Katz, William Loren. *The Black West.* New York:

Katz, William Loren. *Eyewitness: The Negro in American History.* New York: Putnam, 1967.
Doubleday/Anchor, 1987.

Leckie, William H. *The Buffalo Soldiers.* Norman: University of Oklahoma Press, 1967.

Leckie, William H. *The Military Conquest of the Southern Plains.* Norman: University of Oklahoma Press, 1963.

Lee, Irwin. *Negro Medal of Honor.* New York: Dodd Mead, 1967.

Lewis, Francis E. *Negro Army Regulars in the Spanish-American War: Smoked Yankees at Santiago de Cuba.* M.A. thesis, University of Texas, Austin, 1969.

Lynk, Myles. *The Black Troopers or the Daring Heroism of the Negro Soldiers in the Spanish-American War.* New York: AMS, 1971.

Millis, Walter. *The Martial Spirit.* Boston: Little, Brown, 1931.

Muller, William G. *The Twenty-fourth Infantry.* Fort Collins, Colo.: Old Army Press, 1972.

Nalty, Bernard C. *Strength for the Fight.* New York: Collier Macmillan, 1986.

Nankivell, John H. *The Twenty-fifth Infantry.* Fort Collins, Colo.: Old Army Press, 1972.

Stewart, Paul W., and Ponce, Wallace Yvonne. *Black Cowboys.* Broomfield, Colo.: Phillips Publishing, 1986.

Washington, William George. *A History of the Negro Troops in the War of the Rebellion, 1861–1865.* New York: Harper and Brothers, 1888.